MW01109518

JESUS

OR

CHRIST

?

HOWARD M. SNIDER, Ph. D.

Copyright © 2007 by Howard M. Snider, Ph. D.

ISBN 0-7414-3908-5

Published by:

PUBLISHING.COM

1094 New DeHaven Street, Suite 100
West Conshohocken, PA 19428-2713
Info@buybooksontheweb.com
www.buybooksontheweb.com
Toll-free (877) BUY BOOK
Local Phone (610) 941-9999
Fax (610) 941-9959

Printed in the United States of America

Printed on Recycled Paper

Published March 2007

Other books by the author

The Cultural Creation of Christianity

TABLE OF CONTENTS

Religious literature tends to be mythological. These stories illustrate the ways in which human beings struggle with the imponderables of the supernatural world and the meaning of life in this world.

Egyptian religion recognized the intrusion of the supernatural world into this world in the form of God-men who performed many functions for human beings in this life and the life beyond death.

The orderly precession of the equinoxes through the constellations of Taurus, Aries, Pisces and ultimately Aquarius proved the absolute dependability of the heavenly powers and the possibilities of healing, hope and re-creation through the endless cycles of life, death, rebirth and renewal.

The Hebrews formulated stories as they struggled to create an identity. The stories promised property, progeny and power under a special arrangement with their own unique God. They developed stories of special selection, inevitable salvation and finally a Messiah who would actualize their hopes.

By the first century CE an amalgam of Egyptian, Chaldean, Greco-Roman and Jewish cultures enriched the philosophical and religious thought of Saul of Tarsus and his compatriots. Varying interpretation of the ancient myths helped them formulate the myths which attracted followers.

Saul of Tarsus, well acquainted with the God-men of antiquity, at first found the followers of Jesus a threat to religious orthodoxy and social stability. Finally, after much turmoil he concluded that Jesus was a God-man for his age. A Messiah for all people.

Paul wrote letters in which he described Jesus as a Christ. He laid on Jesus all the characteristics and functions of the Christs of Antiquity. Other materials in the NT were written by Christians who followed Paul's theology and elaborated the Christ features.

The leaders of the early church emphasized the uniqueness of Christianity and gradually transformed the Jesus Christ of Paul into a singular, exclusive and literal Christ thereby repudiating the Christs of antiquity.

The church fathers defined what was true and what was false. This truth they encapsulated in Creeds which became the touchstone of orthodoxy. Only those who believed as they believed would go to heaven.

The promoters of Jesus <u>the</u> Christ suppressed all other interpretations and knowledge with tragic consequences for learning and freedom.

A description of possible responses to this book.

Acknowledgments

The people who have helped me are innumerable. For sixty years many have listened to my thoughts which took book form in *The Cultural Creation of Christianity* in 2005. That book raised new questions for me and engendered much conversation with valued friends. These experiences have posed hypotheses and stimulated research and thought. This book includes the revision of some previous ideas and a number of crucial new ones. Some people have read extensive portions of the text of this book and made helpful suggestions. A few went beyond the obligations of friendship and helped with major criticism. Primary among these are: Norman Deckert, Walter Jost, Merrill Raber, Tom Sawin and Hartzel Schmidt. My daughter, Vada Snider, provided invaluable help in editorial work and observations which provided inspiration for new directions at a number of points.

The "Edmonton Group" is always in the background.

Thanks to all of you.

Howard M. Snider
January 2007

Preface

Very little is ever new in any culture. Most of the ways of living and thinking can be traced to ancestors. This is also true of the religious institution and its doctrines, practices and scriptures. The _Holy Bible_ is a compendium of literature which reflects the ways of living and thinking of the peoples of the Near East spanning some centuries on either side of 0 CE (Common Era). These ways of thinking were themselves influenced by earlier ways of living and thinking.

In an attempt to understand this literature it is necessary to ask questions such as the following: What was the worldview of the people who created the oral stories of early religious thought? In what way did the experiences of succeeding generations modify the stories and their meanings? What happened to the myths and their meanings as they moved across cultural boundaries and through long periods of time? What was the cultural background and experience of the people who wrote the materials we read in the Bible? What were the cultural experiences, motivations and purposes of the people who formed early Christianity? Of particular interest in this book is the role of Saul of Tarsus in the formation of theological ideas that gave rise to Christianity in the last half of the first century CE.

Serious consideration of these questions may enrich our understanding of the Christian scriptures and the scriptures of other religions. Inevitably we build on the understandings and beliefs of our ancestors. But how do we proceed with this task?

It is hard work. It is painful work. The pain arises when deeply-held convictions are questioned. For those who think the Bible is history, the certainties of faith may be challenged. To realize that the "Holy Scriptures" and the early church were social creations may be unsettling. For those who have casually discarded religion and think that myths are meaningless these questions may call for re-engagement, a humbling experience.

To begin this task we may have to acknowledge that religious literature is literature. The Greco-Roman world preserved and modified vast collections of religious literature from Persian, Egyptian and other cultures. This wealth of scriptures describes and illustrates the worldview of Near Eastern peoples at the turn of our era. The task of this book is the reconstruction of that social world and its theological perspectives.

This is a scientific task. The coalescence of data into some patterned form enables the creation of hypotheses. This is a challenging and exhilarating activity. Supporting data may be found in subsequent social formations of all kinds.

I am aware of the hypothetical nature of some of the crucial observations in this book. I am also aware of considerable substantiating data which lead to conclusions consistent with sociological theory and the canons of literary criticism. It is my conviction that contradictory evidence will be hard to find.

Howard M. Snider
January 2007

AN INTRODUCTION:

A PRELIMINARY SUMMARY

The belief systems of antiquity are expressed in the stories and myths of the great civilizations of the past. Although there are regional differences the fundamental import of the stories are similar.

The early chapters in this book summarize the central beliefs of the Egyptian, Persian-Chaldean and Hebrew traditions. These civilizations celebrated the powers of the supernatural world and understood the sun, moon and stars to be revelations of that world.

The myths describe the intrusion of supernatural powers into this world. The forms of the intrusion were various. In some cases the fraternization of the Gods with humans produced God-men. The most important of these were "anointed ones."

These "messenger" God-men took care of people and social groups. They were involved in the life of human beings. They encountered other supernatural powers, some of which were evil. Conflicts occurred and the God-men suffered death or dissolution in various ways. But they were always resurrected and restored to life. They subsequently returned to the supernatural world where they had significant roles as they accompanied human beings through death. At the right hand of their Father they functioned as advocates for human beings as they were initiated into the spiritual and eternal family of the Gods.

It was an amalgamation of these belief systems that provided the worldview of the people who lived in Asia Minor and Palestine in the first century of our era.

Associated with these philosophical and religious propositions was a system of social morality inherited particularly from Greco-Roman versions of Persian and Egyptian thought and practice. A strict observance of prescribed hierarchical relationships was essential to stability in society. Obedience, honor, respect, self-control, restraint and, in the Roman legions, celibacy were the marks of the rejuvenated honorable moral man.

It was this general worldview and moral system that characterized the best of Roman citizens. Saul of Tarsus was such a citizen and was at home in this intellectual and moral milieu.

Jesus, the itinerant teacher, preacher and peasant philosopher, rejected this system of thought and substituted a radically different moral code. Jesus advocated love as the way to positive and redeeming relationships. He promoted equality rather than hierarchical control as the way to social order.

Saul did not know Jesus, but he did know Jesus' followers. He knew them and feared them because they advocated a moral and social system that threatened the basis of his religion and the social order of his Roman civilization. How dare Jesus, a fellow Jew, an unsophisticated peasant tradesman, challenge the social system which gave them and their fellow Jews relative peace in a turbulent world?

But Saul's efforts to wipe out the "Jesus followers" failed. Saul, in the frustration of this failure, was forced to reassess his conception of Jesus. It finally dawned on him that Jesus might be another God-man; a God-man for the new age. Finally convinced of this reality he promoted Jesus as the Messiah, a messenger from the supernatural world, a new God-man, a Christ for his age.

The concept of Jesus as a God-man fitted well into Saul's integrated Greco-Roman-Jewish philosophical system. He spent the rest of his life promoting this marvelous discovery, this astounding theological insight. The churches that he founded were based on this doctrine. The letters he wrote described Jesus as a God-man, a Christ, with all the characteristics of the messenger God-men of antiquity.

Succeeding generations rooted in aspects of Paul's theology isolated Jesus from all the other God-men of antiquity and made him unique, singular and exclusive. Thus "**Jesus a Christ**" of Paul's discovery became "**Jesus the Christ**" of fourth century Christianity. In this process the church fathers turned the characteristics and functions of the mythical God-men into literal characteristics and functions. They converted myth into history.

The Christ Saul discovered, rather than Jesus, was the essential figure in the emergence of the Christian church. The hierarchical structures of the Roman Empire rather than Jesus' principles of love and equality became the model for church administration and Christian morality. By the fifth century Jesus had essentially disappeared from Christianity and humanity entered the dark ages.

CHAPTER 1

THEOLOGY AND MYTHOLOGY

The religious and philosophical systems of the ancient world were inspired by and associated with the heavens in a variety of ways. The heavenly bodies: sun, moon and stars in their various formations and conjunctions were, for the civilizations of antiquity, the representations and revelations of the supernatural world.

The Nature of Revelation in Antiquity

The heavens and the regions beyond were, for early Egyptian philosophers and theologians, the realm of the supernatural. It was the domain of Neteru, the primal cause of everything. These powers were the creators of the Gods and spirits who then were instrumental in the creation of the heavenly bodies, the earth and all of nature including human beings.

The powers of the universe, the Gods and the spirits were invisible. But the sun, moon and stars were visible and awe inspiring. They were the manifestation of the powers, Gods and spirits lying behind all creation and all subsequent events. They were revelations of all aspects of the supernatural world. In some ways and in some myths the heavenly bodies were the very Gods themselves.

The people of antiquity searched that complex and enthralling revelation with an intensity and conviction equal to any research activities exhibited by scientists, biblical scholars, theologians and philosophers of our day.

Events of nature and life experiences were understood as the interplay of supernatural forces and the realities in this world. The spirits and Gods had access to the earth and related in many ways to all phenomena occurring here. Thinkers in all societies contemplated these relationships and developed explanations for them. As a result of their work a large body of "knowledge" was accumulated.

Myths were the artistic adaptations of these intellectual constructs. They provided form and vitality to the explanations developed by philosophers and theologians. They were the vehicles by which knowledge was communicated to the masses by storytellers and religious functionaries.

This knowledge, these worldviews, enabled people to structure societies which made human social life possible. This body of knowledge provided explanations for expected and unexpected events. It provided hints and guides for life. The very nature of life, fate and the future were forever at stake in the relationships of humans with the Gods.

On the surface, with our mindset and a superficial reading, many of the myths and stories are absurd, fantastic and even utter nonsense. But read as guides to life in societies of past ages, they provide insight into the deepest of human experience, emotions and relationships. They are stories which plumbed the deepest elements of life as people tried to understand themselves and the imponderables which are beyond the ken of any and all of us. This is the stuff of myth. It is worlds apart from foolishness. The events in the stories never happened in any real sense. But they are symbolic descriptions of common human experiences, expectations and hopes.

Through the centuries many such stories circulated, first in oral form and ultimately in written form. Undoubtedly, through the centuries, many were lost and others deliberately destroyed but we still have a rich library of myths in numerous versions.

It is such interesting and insightful literature we find in the *Pyramid Texts*, the *Egyptian Book of the Dead*, the *Enuma Elish*, the *Gilgamish Epic* of Chaldea, the *AVesta* of Persia and the *Old Testament* of Hebrew culture. Many other myths were produced in the ancient Near East. Homer in Greece and Ovid of the Roman era are two who wrote, collected, compiled and often revised the myths and stories which comprise some of the literary riches of antiquity and the more recent Greco-Roman world. All of these provide us with a sense of the philosophical, theological and religious world in the centuries BCE (Before the Common Era) and are crucial to an understanding of the thought systems and the literary materials associated with the cultural creation of Christianity.

What do these stories really mean and what are they saying? Can they help us understand the worldview and theology of those who were instrumental in the formation of Christianity? Might these ancient myths help us to understand our world and our religion?

The Supernatural World interacts with Our World

As a beginning point let us grant the thinkers of antiquity their fundamental premise; the supernatural world interacts with this world in many ways. It communicates, at the highest level, with human beings through messengers. These representatives came in various forms and performed a range of functions. In a simplistic way they might be understood within two categories. They were either spirits or deities.

Spirits had specific duties relative to humans and nature. They functioned according to specific principles in the same way we understand scientific laws. Thus it was possible for humans to enter into contract relationships with them. If the human obligations such as rituals, incantations and sacrifices were properly performed the spirits responded positively. Failure to do so could result in poor crops, illness and other physical and social misfortunes. But proper and precise performance of these services was always difficult; therefore the response of the spirits was always problematic.[1]

Deities were a different class of supernatural beings. They had a wide range of powers. Theologians and philosophers in the civilizations of antiquity described in marvelous detail the characteristics, behaviors, functions and activities of deities and gave them names. An understanding of these deities and the ways in which they interacted with this world was of crucial importance to human beings.

Gods had characteristics like human beings. They had feelings, emotions and free will. Therefore they were changeable, unpredictable and prone to arbitrary action. Social interaction between humans and the Gods conditioned the benefits which the Gods provided. Poor relationships could have disastrous consequences. The relationship between the Israelites and Jehovah (JHWH) (Yahweh) might be a familiar example of this phenomenon.

In our civilization we think we know the laws of interaction which govern and control the physical and social world. We have our theories and laws derived either from scientific methodology or philosophical and religious belief systems. We act in accord with these hypotheses, theories and laws. The ancients likewise had hypotheses, theories and "laws" by which they lived. These provided the worldview within which generations of people have lived out their lives.

Humans, whether living then or now, are concerned with well-being. Life is complex and mystifying. Humans want insight; they need to know how to relate to the world of nature and their social world. Many are also concerned with the super-natural world and its powers.

4

Knowledge of the Supernatural World

The word "supernatural" refers to something which is above the natural. By the most elemental observation human beings are natural. If we are not natural we are unnatural which is quite different than supernatural. All human beings from the most illiterate cave dwellers of ancient times to the most sophisticated academician or theologian in our modern world are on an even plain when it comes to knowledge of a supernatural world.

From whence then comes all the "knowledge" which many people have of the supernatural world. What is the nature of that "knowledge?"

Humans have a strong need to know the unknowable. We have intense proclivities to explain the unexplainable, to comprehend the incomprehensible. We feel uncomfortable until we fit everything into some consistent structure. The very integrity of our being requires a unification of everything including the unknown.

It is this human characteristic which drives all hypothesizing in the sciences and all speculation in other methods of explanation.

Questions relative to the supernatural are inevitable. Attempts to answer them are also inevitable and it is here where imagination structures explanations for the unexplainable, fabricates knowledge about the unknowable and generates conceptions for the inconceivable. After weighing the "evidence" we manage to make things fit a pattern which is relatively satisfying in both an intellectual and emotional way. When things fit together we have a belief system.

The propositions, doctrines and dogmas which we knit together to produce belief systems are often classified as "knowledge," sometimes even as "revelations," and in orthodox religious systems as "truth." If this kind of knowledge is accepted as an actual representation of the supernatural, such mental activity is sometimes called "faith."

The people of antiquity believed in the "truth" of their myths. But in this they were no different than people in the modern world who have constructed "knowledge" of the unknowable and live by that knowledge. Humans often claim that this kind of "knowledge" comes from the supernatural world and is revealed by "messengers."

Messengers from the Supernatural World

It is not surprising that messenger deities in mythology were high in the cosmic order of things. The term "messenger" translates to Avatar in Persian tradition, Messiah in Hebrew tradition, Christos in Greek tradition and Christ in the English language. These terms refer to a class of sacred phenomena experienced in similar ways in different cultures.

These messengers appeared most frequently at transition points in the life of human beings. They stood at the crossroads of human experience and provided insight into the past. They provided enlightenment at the entrance to new ages, new eras, new years, new days and new experiences. They provided explanations of events in the life of human beings and on occasion informed humans of events to come. In addition to being messengers they performed functions useful for human beings.

The messengers took a form and name appropriate to the culture to which they came. Hence there are variations. A short list would include, Chrishna in Vedic culture, Horus in Egyptian culture, Enurata in Chaldean-Babylonian culture, Mithras in Persian culture, Hermes in Greek culture, Mercury in Roman culture, Messiah in Hebrew culture, Jesus Christ in Christian culture and, from some perspectives, Mohammed in Muslim culture. These messengers brought messages from the supernatural world. They performed many functions for humans, particularly as humans made the transition from this world to the supernatural world.

But what relationship did the "messenger Gods" have with other Gods and the human beings to whom they brought messages. They are almost invariably described as sons-of-God. What does this mean? In what way are they sons of God?

A Genealogy of the Gods

The parentage of sons and daughters of the Gods is extremely complex in the myths of antiquity.

Some sons of God sprang full blown from the Gods and seem to have no mother. These sons of God come by monogenesis and are sometimes described in the scriptures of various cultures as "only begotten" sons. In one edition of the Athenian myth, Cecrops the founder of Athens simply emerged from the earth. In the writings of Ovid the erstwhile, God-man Ericthonius had his birth without a mother. Enkidu, in the Gilgamish epic, became a God in animal form without birth but later became human.[2] In some versions they simply emerged from a rock or from a cave, an explanation very similar to the Arunta myths of Australia or some interpretations of the significance of the ceremonial centers deep in the caves of Lascaux in France.

A second group of sons of God are the sons of Gods and Goddesses. There are many of these named and described in the myths of the ancient world. They persist in folklore and in modified forms in medieval literature.

A third group of sons of God or daughters of God are the progeny of Gods and humans. Most frequently they are children of male Gods and human females.[3] Among the many in Egyptian mythology and one of great relevance for

7

Hebrew theology was the God Thoth who is reported to have fathered a God-man, Thothmoses.[4] Mithras the central figure in the roots of Western Mithraism was the son of the Persian God Ahura Mazda and a human virgin Anahita. The Book of Genesis reports "The sons of God came into the daughters of men and they bore children to them" (Genesis 6:2-4). These children, these God-men were "mighty men," "men of renown," or "heroes." In Christian literature the pregnancy of Mary provides the most classic example. "She was found to be with child of the Holy Ghost."[5] Another version of the same example declares "the Holy Spirit will come upon you and the power of the most High will overshadow you; therefore the child that will be born will be called Holy."[6] There are innumerable examples of this phenomenon in the mythologies of many cultures.

A fourth group are sons of human parentage who are elevated to divine status by an act of the Gods. An interesting example is the Gilgamesh Epic deluge hero Zisuthrus (the earlier Babylonian version of the Hebrew Noah) who with his wife and daughter after leaving the ark on a mountain were transformed to live with the Gods.[7]

These sons of God have the capacity to appear in various forms; frequently as animal, half animal-half human or fully human. They may change form at will or be changed in form by the act of more powerful Gods. God-men can transition to the status of Gods. The New Testament in some contexts declares that Jesus Christ is God. The early church by the fifth century declared in its creeds that Jesus Christ was "God of very God."

These few observations indicate the complexity of the literature and beliefs about the Gods, spirits and powers of the supernatural world and their interactions with this world. The myths concerning messenger God-men were particularly relevant to the common theological understandings at the time of the emergence of Christianity. As we try to understand some forms of Christianity in our day it may be helpful to realize that these theological ideas are still very much alive.

Myths and Truth

The earliest forms of the myths most relevant to the western world had their origins in early Egypt and regions of the Near East. The similarities from myth to myth might indicate a common source. At the very least they reflect common answers to the common ultimate questions which humans ask as they face the vast unknowns about life, the universe and their fate in it.

The answers for the people of antiquity made life possible in their communities, in their time and their place. Many of their answers may seem strange to us but we must understand the meaning of their stories if we are to understand their societies and the world they bequeathed to us. There is no doubt that elements of their myths are perpetuated in our civilization. Therefore it is crucial to understand their myths if we are to understand our myths and the way in which they inform and form our lives.

Myths have intimate connections with ultimate meanings. Theologizing then is the activity by which myths are constructed and the means by which they might be modified to respond to societal needs in different times and circumstances. Thinkers provide explanations of the relationship between things, including human relationships to the world of the unknown. Artists cast these explanations into literary forms which make such conceptions available to the masses.

The masses of the people simply accept the myths promoted by the powerful people in their social group. These myths are accepted as explanations of reality. Over time, even a very short time such as a generation or two, myths become traditional, are perceived as truth, religion promotes them as revelations from the Gods and thus they become sacred.

With such massive social confirmation, myths become powerful forces in shaping the worldview of succeeding generations.

New Myths and Social Change

But inevitably societal conditions change. The myths which supported the ancestors in their circumstances no longer provide adequate explanations for people in new times and new conditions. Crises of explanation and identity emerge. Societies enter a period of turmoil. We live in a time in which traditional societies are encountering western-style mores and as a consequence many societies are in turmoil. Even in western societies environmental and social conditions never before experienced are producing anxiety and are threatening traditional ways of thinking and living.

In these conditions a segment of society will struggle to conserve the old myths. These people believe that the old myths had produced the golden days of their fanciful remembrances and perceptions of earlier times. These people are anxious and see a revitalization of the old myths as the means to recreate the good old days and escape contemporary crises. However the agonizing effort to force the application of old myths in new situations only exacerbates the crises. The old explanations explain nothing about the new situation. New myths must be found or the society will disappear. The scrap heap of history has many examples.

New myths which make sense of new situations are difficult to formulate. Sometimes it does occur and when it does theologizing is at the core of the process. Any new enduring myth will have characteristics of the ultimate and the universal.

New messengers are crucial to new myths. They will ordinarily be flayed, suppressed and effectively killed. But all surviving myths have resurrected messengers. The message will eventually be heard and the people saved. Jesus was this kind of messenger. He rejected the ineffective myths of the Judeo-Greco-Roman world of Palestine. He advocated the myth of love as the way to freedom and security.

Our current world seems guided by the myth: "Violence produces freedom and security." But this myth no longer works. it is doubtful if it ever did. It is a myth which produces suffering, disaster and insecurity. It makes all men slaves to fear. It is time for this failed myth to be discarded.

It is time to take the stories of Jesus seriously. It is time to learn the lessons of love. It is time to engage in the kind of life which turns enemies into friends. It is time to identify with all people and recognize that we are brothers and sisters in one human race. This is the core of Jesus' kind of Christianity.

CHAPTER 2

EGYPTIAN THEOLOGY

Egyptian hieroglyphics from tombs, pyramids, temples, vast public buildings, and diverse forms of scriptures on Papyrus and Vellum from archeological sites, have been translated and compiled in a number of forms. In a summary way many of these writings can best be described as liturgical materials for use in funeral rites. They have theological references and provide a description of Egyptian deities with their numerous names, roles, functions and relationships.

Humans and Gods in the Cycle of Life, Death and New Life

Even a cursory acquaintance with these materials suggests two realities about Egyptian theology. Contrary to stereotypes of Egyptian culture there is not a fixation with death. There is rather a remarkable emphasis on life; this life and the future life. Wallis Budge made a translation of the _Papyrus of Ani_, a manuscript from about 240 BCE and entitled his work "_The Book of the Dead_."[8] The _Papyrus of Ani_ itself was a translation of Egyptian materials from about 1600 BCE and earlier. In its earlier form it was known as the _Chapters of Coming Forth by Day_.[9]

The materials known as the _Pyramid Texts_[10] were pronouncements and ritual incantations used at the funerals of the Pharaohs as early as 3100 BCE.[11] Some of these materials were incorporated in the Egyptian _Book of the Dead_.[12]

The basic message of these materials may be summarized in the observation: "Humans may die. But they die to this life only to be born again to a new day and a new life in company with the spiritual powers and Gods of the universe."

The transition from life in this world to life in the supernatural world is an ultimate crucial event. The ceremonies and rites associated with this transition are the events in which the messengers from the supernatural world are remarkably active. It is life and the preparation for transition to life with the Gods which is the focus of funerary rites, not death.

Life in this world is important but it is only one phase in the ongoing cycle of life, death and new life. The deities and God-men from the supernatural world are involved with humans at all times. In this world their functions are oriented toward social stability and the ongoing cycles of life as these are preliminary to the stable and enduring spiritual life in the supernatural world.

Although there are innumerable Gods named in the Egyptian pantheon they are all interconnected and even inter-changeable. This hint at monotheism seems to have been promoted by Pharaoh Akhenaten.

Let us remember that these Gods are not historical figures. They are timeless mythological actors in stories which helped humans probe, explain and understand the meaning of their existence at the deepest level.

With this background let us look at a few manifestations of the supernatural world as it intruded into the Egyptian world. There are innumerable myths of various kinds, but there are a few myths which seem to summarize the fundamental thought of Egyptian culture in a comprehensive way.

The Osiris/Horus Myth

The story of Horus, the most common and probably the most important myth, appears in a multitude of variations through thousands of years in Egyptian scriptures. The central figures: Re, Ra, Osiris, Horus and Isis (the major female deity) have distinct characteristics but are functionally interchangeable. These deities seem to be regional expressions of a common mythological reality. They are at times even confused with the Neteru who are preliminary to everything because they exist without beginning or end.

There are numerous sources for the crucial elements of the Horus Myth.[13] The following itemized paragraphs summarize its central features.

1. Ra the supreme sun God[14] had a son Osiris, another son Seth, a daughter Isis and numerous other progeny. Horus was the son of Osiris and Isis.

2. In the complex of Egyptian scriptures Horus is one of the prominent figures. He is a composite God who incorporates many Gods including his own father and even Ra the father of them all. His body parts, arms, legs etc. are sometimes described as Gods. In some senses, in spite of the complexity of names and functions there seems to be a single supernatural power with many characteristics and functions.

3. Different names seem to be associated with specific functions. Osiris for example is associated with the male aspect of regeneration in nature and is also the God of the setting sun, the end of life and thus also the God of the dead. Horus, among a multitude of other functions, is a victor over evil, an anointed one, a messenger to humans, a God-man and in the final end of things an advocate for humans at their entrance into supernatural life.

4. In the Egyptian social system the pharaohs were incarnations of these Gods and thus were sons of God,

15

anointed ones and God-men. No real distinction could be made between Horus and the Pharaoh. Through centuries and succeeding dynasties there were many pharaohs, therefore many Horus incarnations and thus many God-men.[15]

5. The life and death of Horus in one Pharaoh and resurrection in the next represented the cyclical events of both the celestial and natural worlds. It symbolized the constant repetition of the ongoing cycles of life. It provided hope for the repetition of the necessary events of human existence. It guaranteed security and continuity of all that really mattered.

6. Although there was one Horus there were many. The constant reincarnation of Horus provided social stability, social rejuvenation and constant predictable relationships with nature and the supernatural world.

7. The ultimate super powers of the universe are referred to as "Pyramid builders" with many references to their characteristics and functions relative to human beings and Egyptian society. These superpowers placed their monuments, the pyramids, on earth among their dependants. The pyramids were reminders of the supernatural powers but were also resting places for the pharaohs who incarnated and symbolized those powers. The pyramid tunnels represent the passage ways from earth to the domain of the Gods.[16]

8. Horus is symbolized in a number of ways. He is pictured as a child on the lap of Isis often with royal robes. He is pictured as an emblazoned sun, a figure whose head is surrounded by a marvelous halo. Thus he is the source of light and life. He is commonly symbolized as a falcon-headed God who soars into the heavens and is the God of wisdom, insight and enlightenment.

9. Seth, a brother of Osiris, is an evil antagonist, a symbol of darkness and chaos. In most versions of the myth they engage in a struggle to the death. Osiris is killed, his body is dismembered and its parts scattered.[17]

10. Isis, becoming aware of this horrendous event, anxiously searches through the land for her husband. She with the help of Horus finally recovers and reassembles the body parts. Through this reconstitution and resurrection the restoration of life occurs.[18]

11. Horus avenges his father's death by encountering and defeating Seth. In some versions this is an ongoing and repeated action assuring the society that evil will always ultimately be defeated.[19]

12. By these means evil, darkness and chaos are overcome. Life, light and enlightenment are restored with each new day, each new year, each new pharaoh and each new dynasty. There is always light after darkness. There is always spring after winter. There is always life after death. These events do not happen automatically. The deities and representative God-men are instrumental in all these reassuring events of life.

13. Osiris-Horus is the victor over evil and thus a savior.[20]

14. In some versions Horus is pictured with two eyes representing the sun and moon. As day ends light fades or when the new moon occurs Horus is blinded, chaos and confusion reigns. What is cause and effect? Horus is the bringer of light. He is the anointed one who enlightens all men coming into this world. The cycle of life, death and life is in the hands of the Gods and they are forever true. Humans may rest in this security.

15. Osiris after his reconstitution and resurrection is transported to the supernatural world where he becomes one

with the Gods. He is initiated into the presence of Ra the sun God where he stands or sits at his father's right hand.[21] Horus replaces Osiris as the more prominent God on earth.

16. Osiris and Horus are variously represented as responsible for the transportation of humans to the supernatural world.

17. In the supernatural world humans are ushered into the hall of Maat (measure or rule) where a panel of judges makes an assessment of their deeds while on earth. Two categories of behavior are judged. One is the nature of interrelationships with fellow human beings while on earth; a set of ethical and moral criteria. The second relates to the ways humans reverenced the Gods.

The following testimony, of an Egyptian nobleman, found in the *Papyrus of Ani*, illustrate these categories.[22]

"I have not committed sins against men. I have not opposed my family and kinsfolk. I have not acted fraudulently in the Seat of Truth. I have not known men who were of no account. I have not wrought evil. I have not made it to be the first [consideration daily that unnecessary] work should be done for me. I have not brought forward my name for dignities. I have not [attempted] to direct servants [I have not belittled God]. I have not defrauded the humble man of his property. I have not done what the Gods abominate. I have not vilified a slave to his master. I have not inflicted pain. I have not caused anyone to go hungry. I have not made any man to weep. I have not committed murder. I have not given the order for murder to be committed. I have not caused calamities to befall men and women. I have not plundered the offerings in the temples. I have not defrauded the Gods of their cake-offerings. I have not carried off the fenkhu cakes [offered to] the Spirits. I have not committed fornication. I have not masturbated [in the sanctuaries of the God of my city]. I have not diminished from the bushel. I have not filched [land from my neighbour's estate and] added it to my

own acre. I have not encroached upon the fields [of others].
I have not added to the weights of the scales. I have not
depressed the pointer of the balance. I have not carried away
the milk from the mouths of children. I have not driven the
cattle away from their pastures. I have not snared the geese
in the goose-pens of the Gods. I have not caught fish with
bait made of the bodies of the same kind of fish. I have not
stopped water when it should flow. I have not made a cutting
in a canal of running water. I have not extinguished a fire
when it should burn. I have not violated the times [of
offering] the chosen meat offerings. I have not driven away
the cattle on the estates of the Gods. I have not turned back
the God at his appearances. I am pure. I am pure. I am
pure."

18. In some versions Horus then ushers the humans who
have satisfied the criteria in the hall of Maat into the
presence of his father Osiris. He then stands or sits at the
right hand of his father and acts as an advocate for the
humans who desire to become a son or daughter of Osiris
and thus a spiritual being, a child of God and the brother or
sister of Horus.

19. The name Horus appears in the rituals related to the
opening of the mouth of Osiris. He is a messenger and
carries the message of his father. [23]

20. The eye of Horus is a common symbol in pictographic
script. This aspect of the myth describes the eye, a single eye
in this case, as shattered and the pieces scattered and then
gathered and reconstituted. This is obviously another version
of the scattering of the parts of Osiris and his reconstitution.
The eye of Horus is sometimes identified with the lunar
cycle and the transition from the darkness of the new moon
to the full orbed light of the full moon. It is thus the eye of
the sky. According to Mercer, it represents wholeness and
health. The symbol for the eye of Horus was modified over

centuries and today appears on physician's prescription forms all over the world as Rx.[24]

21. The characteristics and functions of Egyptian deities are even more numerous than their names. These characteristics and functions appear in the theologies of later civilizations and are attached to other names. Obviously it is the actions and characteristics of the Gods and God-men that is important and not their names.

Characteristics applied to Gods and God-men

Budge in his work *The Book of the Dead* (Budge 1895), finds dozens of references to the names and functions of God-men and deities in Ancient Egyptian mythology. The following list of terms and descriptions, found widely dispersed in that literature, are collected here to show the diversity of conceptions which the peoples of antiquity attributed to their God-men.

A short list of characteristics and names would include the following: First born. Beginning of being. Self begotten. Self produced. Self created. Father of Fathers. Father from the beginning. God of Gods. Lord of the Earth. Lord of eternity. Judge of the dead.

A short list of activities and functions would include the following: Maker of the Gods. Stretched out the heavens. Creator of men seated at a potters wheel fashioning a human being. Holds in his hands emblems of power, sovereignty and rule. Established unending and unvarying right and truth upon the earth. He holds the emblem of water in his hands. Depicted in the form of a man he wears the crowns, and holds the sceptre and the emblem of life. He vanquished night and darkness. He typified the light. Osiris was chosen as a type of what the deceased hoped to become. His glorified body should enter into his presence in heaven.

Osiris seems to have incorporated most of these characteristics and functions. Budge summarizes this idea in the following quotation, "He (Osiris) became the type of eternal existence and the symbol of immortality; as such he usurped not only the attributes of Ra but those of every other God." In a comprehensive summary of the Osiris-Horus myth Budge observes, "The ceremonies connected with the events of the suffering, death and resurrection of Osiris occupied a very prominent part in the religious observance of the Egyptians."

Egyptian Culture had longterm influences

The Egyptian culture endured for many thousands of years. The people who became known as Israelites emerged from tribal groups in the regions of the Near East which were extensively influenced by Egyptian culture. It is no accident that the Hebrew Scriptures are replete with reflections, inferences, intimations and direct parallels from those influences.

Tribal and national cultures of the Near East and later even the great Greek and Roman Empires in their far-flung reaches inherited many elements from Egyptian sources. One of the remarkable legacies was the presence of the cult of Isis in the Roman Empire. This cult persisted with temples and ceremonies into the fifth century CE.[25]

Cultures do cross fertilize. National and tribal boundaries never were and never can be barriers to communication and the transmission of ideas. Consequently deities similar to Egyptian deities with modified functions and different names existed in many cultures. This was true of Persian culture more than a millennia BCE and also true of the great Greco-Roman culture in the first centuries of the CE.

CHAPTER 3

PERSIAN THEOLOGY

Persian and Assyrian peoples lived in the area of the Middle East we now call Afghanistan, Iran and Iraq. These peoples were contemporary with the middle and later dynasties of Egyptian Pharaohs. They shared much with the Egyptians in their view of this world and the supernatural world. Even their deities, although differing in names, had many similar qualities, characteristics and functions.

However they had some unique conceptions of the supernatural world and its influence on this world. Many of these were developed as early as the second millennium BCE and over time influenced the peoples of surrounding areas, particularly their Indo-European ancestral home to the northwest and later Asia Minor and the Roman Empire. Their myths made a significant contribution to the mix of theologies in the Near East in the time of Saul of Tarsus and the cultural creation of Christianity.[26]

The religious system known as Mithraism was common throughout the Near East.[27] A major version of this philosophical system was Zoroastrianism, named after its principle teacher. There were regional variations and subsets of ideas but the myth of Mithras was the common component.

The origins of this myth are traced by some scholars to ancient Persia as early as two millennia BCE. Some find evidences of Vedic origins.[28] Others contend it was formulated as late as the fourth century BCE in the region of Cilicia in Asia Minor. Despite the disagreements about the time and place of origins there is general agreement that the cult of Mithras was imported into Asia Minor by the Roman legions as the power of Rome displaced Greece. By the turn of our era it was a controlling ideology of the Roman military institution and influential among the political and intellectual elites in the Empire.[29]

The Elements of the Mithras Myth

The name Mithras has a number of variations such as Mithra and Mithri. The characteristics and functions also varied from region to region. As with the Egyptian myths there are many versions. However the significant theological doctrines are common to all versions.[30]

The following items list the basic elements of the myth relevant to the discussion of this chapter.

1. Mithra was born to a human virgin, Anahita. His father was an eastern supreme God Ahura Mazda. Thus Mithras was a God-man.[31]

2. The western Roman versions suggest he burst forth from a rock or an egg.[32] In this version he would be an "only begotten" son of God.

3. The earlier eastern versions indicate the place of birth was a cave or a stable and occurred in the presence of shepherds.[33]

4. The birth was associated with magi and their travels.

5. Mithras in the earliest of the western versions was a God of slaves and freedmen but with the accretion of the title Invictus (victor) he became the God of soldiers.[34] In the Roman version the identification with Sol Invictus the Sun God persisted for centuries.

6. A bull in numerous versions is perceived as a symbol of the sun God and is seen as the source of life for animals and plants.

7. Mithras, in maturity captured a bull and dragged it to his cave where he slaughtered it.[35]

8. The blood from the bull dripped down to the ground and fertilized the earth which then produced new life of all kinds.[36]

9. The new life for human beings was associated with an intense commitment to a moral life.[37]

10. Women were not permitted as members of the Mithraic cults.[38]

From this myth grew an extensive and dynamic philosophical and religious system which endured for centuries in much of the western world. The community of devotees and worshippers revered a central icon, the Tauroctony and participated in a complex ritual known as the Taurobolium. These two features marked Mithraism wherever it appeared.[39]

The Tauroctony symbols and Taurobolium Ceremonies of Mithraism

Ceremonial centers for this philosophical and religious system were established all over the Near East and Europe by the early centuries of the CE. These ceremonial centers, now known as Mithraeums were located in caves or excavated covered sites, such as the catacombs of Rome,[40] an obvious symbolic reference to the cave in which Mithras was initiated into this world.

The icon, the Tauroctony was a pictorial representation of the myth. Carved in stone in each worship site was a scene exhibiting the God-man Mithras grasping the snout of a bull, pulling back its head while he thrusts a dagger into its heart. Blood flows from the fatal wound and drips to the ground and a gutter at the bottom of the scene. In the foreground are a dog, a scorpion and a snake. In the background is a group of men eating and drinking.[41]

This icon is present wherever the community gathered to remember the myth and celebrate its meaning. Remains of these graphic symbols can still be found in the Middle East and Europe as far north as Hadrian's Wall in Great Britain.

The second element was the reenactment of the crucial features of the myth. This was the Taurobolium ritual. In this ritual a bull was slaughtered and the blood was collected. The blood was used in the baptism of initiates into the cult. A symbolic communal meal was celebrated consisting of meat from the bull and a beverage of blood mixed with herbs.

The Meaning of Tauroctony and Taurobolium

What is the meaning of all these gruesome rituals?

What does the communion meal accomplish? From whence did the myth arise? What is the meaning in this myth and these rituals that could incite the interest and ceremonial repetition by people through centuries of time?

Were these people simply crude, barbaric savages deluded by evil spirits and devils? Were they merely our stereotypic primitive men entranced with weird, fantastic esoteric practices?

Let us remember that they were the same kind of people who created vast, sophisticated cultures and remarkable social organizations capable of designing and constructing such wonders of the world as the hanging gardens of Babylon, the complex irrigation systems of Mesopotamia, the ziggurats of the plains and the astounding public works and engineering wonders of great cities.

Probably we should look behind the myth itself to the realities of the world, the universe and the culture in which these people lived. If we do so we will sense again the primal reality experienced by all humans who dare to encounter the imponderable questions of their existence.

These cultures lived close to the physical realities of life. They knew that light and heat came from the sun in the heavens. They knew and felt the turbulence of storms and the refreshing function of rain. They knew they had to work to plant the seeds, fertilize the ground, guide the waters through the irrigation canals, flood the fields and harvest the crops. But regardless of how they planned and worked, nature was unpredictable and they knew they were totally dependent.

The forces which provided the crucial light and heat and the storms which produced the water were obviously at work. How could those forces be induced to provide abundance? How could they be contacted to hear the cries for help at all the crucial points of life? How indeed?! The ancients struggled to answer these questions.

Revelation from the Heavens

Humans of antiquity looked to the heavens for help. Their knowledge was based on solid observations and the answers came in theological form. Thus if we are to understand their life, culture, theology, myths and rituals we must understand their view of the heavens and their expectations of the powers resident there.

The heavenly bodies played a central role in the life and thus in the belief systems of the cultures of the Near East. The sun by day gave light and life and warmth and comfort. The stars and moon were lesser lights but provided guidance and confirmed the certainties of an ordered universe. The heavenly bodies were, for the thinkers of antiquity, the most concrete revelations of the supernatural world available. It was this data which invited the work of thinkers, theologians, philosophers and artists of all kinds.

In our urban life we have become aliens to the heavenly worlds. They have faded in the blur of incandescent lights and the fog of pollution. Most people have lost sight of them as we have lost sight of most elemental aspects of human existence. Astronomers are still interested in the stars as sources of information about the cosmos. A few people are interested in the constellations of the zodiac as they contemplate their horoscope. Most urban dwellers have only the most meager awareness of the stars.

We have trivialized the heavens and put them out of our minds. But the people of the ancient world had a remarkable and vital contact with the heavenly bodies and understood them in dynamic ways.

They related their life to the whole of the universe, this world, the world of the sun, moon and stars and all they represented about a supernatural world. They looked to the celestial world for intimations and revelations relevant to the deepest of human emotional and spiritual needs. They hoped to find in the cosmic forces some explanation for existence, reason for being and hope for the future.

From all of this has grown an extensive body of literature about the heavenly bodies and their meaning with respect to the intersection of our world and the supernatural world.

The Precession of the Equinoxes

At the core of this literature is a rather sophisticated astronomical understanding of the sun and its annular movement through constellations of stars. It was also observed that the moon made exactly the same cycle through the heavens and moved through these same constellations approximately twelve times each year.

The ancients, many centuries BCE, had divided the band of the heavens through which the sun and moon move into twelve or thirteen relatively equal parts, sometimes called houses. They selected constellations of stars, one in each of these parts, and gave some of them the names of earthly creatures. The Greek name for animal is "zoon" and so the band of the heavens where these constellations are located is known as the Zodiac. The center of this band is on the plane of our solar system and is known as the ecliptic.

In addition to all of this there is another astronomical feature even more significant in the formation of the myths of the ancient world, the lore of the Middle East and the symbolism relevant to the beginnings of the Christian church as Saul of Tarsus envisioned it.

The astronomer Hipparchus in the second century BCE explained the precession of the equinoxes, a phenomenon which had been known in a rudimentary way much earlier.

We know this phenomenon now as the wobble of the earth's axis and its effect on the point of the intersection of the ecliptic and the celestial equator. This point moves approximately .014 degrees each year. Thus in 2160 years this point will have moved 30 degrees. In astrological terms it will have moved through one entire house of the zodiac.

The axis of the earth in our time points toward the star we call Polaris. In the future as in the past it will point to different "north stars" as it traces a circular path through the heavens until in 26000 years it will again point to Polaris. The result of this movement causes a precession of the point of the vernal equinox through the twelve houses of the zodiac every 26,000 years. Since there are twelve houses or divisions in the Greek and Roman understanding of the zodiac the equinox will spend approximately 2160 years in each successive house.

This material may be marvelously boring but it is marvelously significant in understanding the intellectual climate and the worldview which provided Saul of Tarsus with his screen of meaning.

The Ages of Taurus, Aries, Pisces and the coming age of Aquarius

More than 2300 BCE the location of the sun at the vernal equinox was in its final years in the constellation Taurus the Bull. This constellation is associated with three other constellations which lie to either side of the zodiac. These three are Canus Major the dog, Hydra the snake and Scorpio the scorpion.[42] These three appear in the tauroctony – the icon of Mithraism.[43]

For the next 2160 years the vernal equinox was in the constellation with the sign of Aries, the Ram or Lamb. At about 60 BCE it moved into the constellation with the sign of Pisces or fish. And now if we look ahead to 2100 CE the sun at the vernal equinox will be entering the constellation with the sign Aquarius. These long periods of time are generally called the age of Taurus, the age of Aries, the age of Pisces and the coming Age of Aquarius.

If one accepts the earliest origins of the myth of Mithras, the astrological age of Taurus the bull was coming to an end. The myth and attendant religious and philosophical systems were directly shaped by this marvelous celestial event. Some scholars date the origin of the myth as late as the fourth century BCE and find it emerging in Asia Minor. If one insists on this later date, a likely possibility, it is a marvelous retroactive explanation of the movement of the heavenly bodies with meaningful significance for the worldview of succeeding generations.

With this background what does the Mithras myth mean and how is it relevant to understanding the cultural context in which Christianity was formed?

Social Stability, Hope and Regeneration

In the first and most obvious way it was a dramatic story revealing the power and consistency of the supreme Gods. It demonstrated their power to move the heavenly bodies in a marvelously precise way. The precession of the equinoxes from the house of Taurus to the house of Aries to the house of Pisces was proof positive that the powers which designed the cosmos were in control. These powers had brought into being the spirits and Gods who had created the universe and who inhabited the heavenly bodies. The universe with its stars in ordered constellations demonstrated the genius of their design and scope of their power. And this power continued endlessly in an undiminished way through eons of time without beginning or end. Mithras, the God-man who represented the supreme beings and the ultimate powers of the universe in slaughtering the bull, symbolized to all people of his day this marvelously consistent control of the changing events through all of time.

For all who understood this myth there was an intellectual and emotional reassurance that beneficent, consistent and never-changing powers were still in control and they need have no fear. The Enneads were without beginning or ending. They were infinitely powerful; they exercised unwavering control and were never-changing. The Gods with endless regularity provided the sustenance of life. In the myth, the blood of the slaughtered bull gushed out onto the ground and symbolized the "masculine essence that fertilized the feminine earth and returned life to the land."[44]

The end of an age symbolized by the slaughter of the bull represents the death of the past and the transition to the new. It symbolizes, at the ultimate cosmic level the complex cyclical realities of nature and life. It represents the passage of day into night, fall to winter, life to death. It symbolizes all the significant transitions which humans experience in this world. Through subsequent centuries the reenactment of the core event of the myth in the Taurobolium and the graphic representation in the Tauroctony reminded people that the universe was stable and the cyclical events of human existence were secure.

This is only the beginning of the significance of this myth. There are two other dimensions which probe the deepest concerns of human beings as they seek for answers to the unanswerable questions of life.

Mithras slaughtered the bull. On the surface it seems to be a drama of ultimate antagonism. But Mithras and the bull are inseparable. It is a unified single event. Mithras the God-man is the incarnation of Sol Invictus, the victorious sun God, the equivalent of Ra in the Egyptian system. Mithras kills the past, spills the blood and thus initiates new life.

In a spiritual sense it symbolizes the death of the old life and the end of all the failures and disappointments which humans encounter in their journey through life. All of the evils are slaughtered. The sins of the past die and pass away and a new beginning can be made. In an Asia Minor version of the Taurobolium ceremony the devotees who wished to be spiritually purified entered a pit covered with a latticework of poles. A bull was slaughtered on this latticework and the blood ran down over the penitents below. The penitents' sins were washed away and they could begin a new life; a life cleansed of past offenses and a life restored to fellowship in the community.

Associated with this newness of life particularly in the Roman legions was a rigorous personal morality. Behavioral characteristics of this morality included: Truth, honor, courage, loyalty, obedience and commitment to contract obligations.[45] This morality was unusually demanding. Self-discipline and self-control were absolutely required behavioral characteristics. Thus a periodic sense of cleansing and renewal was therapeutic.

But is there more? What about the persistent and nagging human questions about death and the future?

A regular prayer in the Taurobolium ceremonies practiced by the devotees of Mithraism was a prayer for rebirth. They prayed, "Spirit of Spirit, if it be your will, lend me immortal life so that I may be reborn, and the sacred spirit breath in me again."[46] The implications of this prayer have been debated. It has been suggested that some followers of the Mithras cult had little concern about a future life. Does the prayer refer only to spiritual rebirth after purification? Does it refer only to the new life in this life after being purified by the blood of the Taurobolium ritual?

Certainly this cosmic myth symbolized a resurrection and a new life. A new birth was sure, a spiritual awakening would ensue. The spiritual powers of the universe would rejuvenate and invigorate life at the deepest spiritual level. A cleansed and purified life unencumbered with the dregs of the past was possible. It was a time for hope.

But there is a hint that the devotees were concerned also about life after death. What is the nature of the anticipated immortality? Given the supernatural dimensions of Greco-Roman culture it is difficult to reject the implication that the prayer refers to a birth into life with the "Spirit of Spirits." Is the washing in the blood a prerequisite for initiation into the eternal supernatural world where "the sacred spirit breathe?"

As the age of Taurus passed, the Age of Aires, the ram or lamb began and represented the passage from night to day and winter to spring. It symbolized the reality of the escape from past failures to a purified life. In the final analysis it ensured the passage from this earthly life to the spiritual life of the supernatural world.

All this was the essence of the myth. All this was pictured in the Tauroctony and was celebrated in the rituals of the Taurobolium.

The continuity of the Myth

Centuries later in a variation of this complex symbolism, the bull with Mithra is an avatar. In a Greek version a white bull is an incarnation of Zeus who with the human Europa fathers a child who begins a new life, a new city and a new kingdom. A white bull, for some Christians, was representative of Christ who carried souls to heaven and thus a symbol of the ultimate transition to new life.[47]

The age of Taurus passed. The age of Aries the ram or lamb endured into the century before the Common Era.

The Hebrews of the Old Testament lived in the age of Aries. It is the death of the lamb and not the death of a bull that is significant in the centuries before the Common Era. The ram or the lamb played a very central role in the religious rituals of Hebrew temple worship and religious thought. A central motif of their sacrificial system entailed the death or abandonment to the desert wilderness of a lamb or ram or goat. This ritual parallels the slaughter of the bull by Mithra and symbolized similar spiritual realities.

These symbols and their meaning were common elements of the cultures of the Near East at the beginning of our era. The rituals are as old as the myths. The ceremonies symbolized the passing of the old, the emergence of the new, the birth of a new life and the revelation of a new creation.[48] At the core of all the myths was the composite avatar, the messenger from the supernatural world.[49]

These rituals and ceremonies have been practiced for many thousands of years. We do so to this day and the meanings are the same. Death occurs but resurrection follows and new life emerges.

Cultures tend to be conservative. Consequently the most important elements of belief systems persist long after the creative periods in which they were formed. This was true of both the Taurus symbol and the Aries symbol. Both were present in the early centuries of the CE and even persist in images and religious language 2000 years later.

The age of Aries passed about 60 BCE. The beginning of the CE then coincided with the early years of the new age of Pisces, the fish.

This also symbolized a time for new things, a time for cleansing and purification, a time for new birth, resurrection, enlightenment and a time for hope. It was a time for the appearance of a new avatar, a new bringer of light, a new messenger. These new things would not be unique but they would be reincarnations of the principles, powers and functions of all preceding God-men, saviors and powers of renewal.

The symbolism of the sacrifice of animals, whether a bull or ram or lamb had deep and fundamental spiritual meaning through centuries. The continuation of this symbolism and the incorporation of their meanings in successive systems of thought is a logical, direct, obvious and inescapable sequel.

This philosophical system was a driving dynamic force in the Roman Empire. It is this kind of thought which comprised the general religious context of Saul and the people who became Christians in the early centuries of our era.

Christianity was not born without a father and a mother. It had a rich and multifaceted ancestry. To understand our religion we must know and appreciate these evolving traditions. Many of the characteristics we find in Christianity can be found in these antecedents. They were obviously present, at least in nascent form, in the belief systems of antiquity and in some cases even fully developed and even richer in form.[50]

As we embrace the emergence of Christianity from its origins in antiquity we may gain a sense of the continuity of this awesome social reality. We have much to gain by seeking to understand the myths of antiquity.

The Hebrew tradition developed in the age of Aries. The wealth of insight from Egyptian and Persian-Chaldean civilizations was crucial in the formation of Hebrew culture. To that background the Hebrews added their own stories. We turn in the next chapter to that material.

CHAPTER 4

HEBREW THEOLOGY

From a Christian point of view the corpus of Hebrew theology is found in the Old Testament. Judaism has additional sources. For the purposes of this book the Old Testament will provide the data. The nature of mythological literature will provide the framework for an understanding of the culture and theology of a people sometimes referred to as "the chosen people" or "God's chosen people," "Israelites," "Hebrews" and, in more recent times, "Jews."

The Old Testament from a Literary Perspective

The literature of the Old Testament is relatively late as religious literature of antiquity goes. In written form the earliest materials did not appear until the seventh or eighth centuries BCE. These scriptures reflect the myths and stories of the oral traditions of particular tribal groups of the Near East. As Hebrew society emerged, modifications were made. These revised myths spoke with poignancy sufficiently unique to create a cohesive minority group within complex and alien societies.

The particular amalgam of thought which underlay Hebrew theology owes much to Persian thought on the one hand and Egyptian thought on the other. The Hebrew Scriptures recognize these sources by reference to the origins of the Israelites and stories of various sojourns through centuries of time in those regions.

Abram, according to the Old Testament narrative, was a native son of Chaldean culture.[51] Thus his worldview was inescapably formulated in that context. His ancestors and his immediate family were familiar with the myths of their homeland.[52] The Gods of that world were their Gods. The creative powers of the supernatural world, the Enneads or the Elohim were the powers which they recognized and to which they referred when they thought about the physical and social world in which they lived.[53]

As time passes and generations come and go, culture and ideas change. The impact of geographical transition, family crises and encounters with numerous alien peoples were factors in the creation of Hebrew culture. To understand this culture and these people it is necessary to understand the stories which undergirded their life. These myths and the reasons for their formulation is the fundamental burden of the Old Testament. Let us begin at the beginning.

Abram and His God

"In the beginning the Gods (Elohim) created the heavens and the earth."[54] This statement is parallel to all the creation myths of antiquity. The variations are inconsequential.

But we are soon into the fundamental explanations of the creation of a people, a society and a culture.

Abram and Lot with their extended families, like their immediate ancestor, left their homeland and moved to a new land.[55]

People in antiquity did not move on a whim. They were tied to their lands and their Gods. However people did move, as we do, with the hope of improving the circumstances of life. Leaving the familiar, uprooting ones household and moving to strange places is an onerous task, fraught with anxiety and stress. It requires great motivation.

When people move they look for signs to justify their move. They seek evidences which support their decisions and plans. They anxiously await those blessings for which they moved. People look outside themselves, even to the supernatural world for support and affirmation. They do this with a conviction that God, the Gods, fate or hard work will provide prosperity and blessings. Abram was no different!

This family from the Ur of Chaldea occupied a niche of land among the Canaanites in the land of Palestine. Abram had moved to a strange land whose people were strange and whose Gods he did not know.

But he had taken his own God with him.

He had moved and survived. This alone was some measure of confirmation that his plans were sanctioned. His God was obviously still with him. His supernatural world was intact. But he hoped for more.

Abram and his God made an agreement. It was a covenant of affinity and exclusiveness. This God promised to provide a vast range of astounding blessings if Abram recognized him as his exclusive God. Abram had a single obligation. He would appeal to no other God and would worship no other God. His God would do all the rest.

This was a remarkably singular and dangerous commitment in a world where multitudes of Gods arranged the affairs and fate of lands and people. Some Gods were attached to geographical places. Other Gods provided an array of services to individuals and groups as they went about their daily life. In the world of antiquity, it was critical to be on good terms with a whole range of deities who in their many roles combined to make life prosperous and pleasant.

Abram was not a monotheist. No one was! To commit oneself to a single God who claimed to be able to do everything and take care of every physical and social need was a proposition that no knowledgeable and practical human in that world would ever contemplate. But all the Gods of the region were strange to Abram.

The Covenant Myths

His own God had come with him. But his God hardly had a name! How much explanation is there in a name like "I am who I am?" Yet this God expected Abram to enter into this astounding contract.

What were the advantages and the consequences of choosing between his God and the Gods of the new land? His God had blessed him thus far, but would he continue such favors in the long run? What would the local Gods and their people do to him? Was his God a long shot in this new setting?

Abram took the dare. He entered into this contract fully aware of its implications. It took astounding faith. The covenant was marked and sealed with the change of his name. Abram became Abraham.

It was an astounding and frightening contract. But the payoff would be great. An exclusive God would make possible the emergence of an exclusive people; his own people!

His God required exclusive recognition and the worship which this implied. Abraham had no other obligations. His God, however, had numerous and marvelous obligations. His God had made promises of a land, innumerable posterity, prosperity and even national power. All this would come from the endless bounty and graciousness of this singular and exclusive God.

The solidification of the covenant was accomplished with the designation of a ceremonial site, the erection of a monument and performance of rituals. It was a place of special remembrance and a place where Abraham and his descendants could encounter their unchanging God.[56]

This complex of behaviors and the formation of supporting myths seem fundamental to the development of group identity and integrity as social groups contemplate the nature of this world and the unknown nature of the supernatural world.

Abraham and his household survived; clear evidence that his God was multifaceted in functions and power. Obviously, for Abraham, his nameless God was superior to all other Gods. This doctrine became a central proposition in Hebrew theology.

The Hebrew people were keenly aware that they lived in a world and a universe of multiple deities and spirits. These deities had characteristics like human beings. They could be angered, appealed to and placated. But Abraham's God was different. He was unchanging and had, it seemed, provided an unconditional covenant.

Abraham and his family celebrated and worshipped. But celebration and worship cannot go on forever and as they turned to the problems of human existence there were realities everywhere. Palestine was not a land flowing with milk and honey. The land was owned and occupied by native Canaanite peoples. Abraham and his family were aliens and an ethnic minority. Prosperity was far away. Power was nowhere in sight.

And where was the evidence of a great people? His wife was barren.

A drought forced him to find sustenance in Egypt. Here a remarkable event reversed his fortune. But it was all based on a lie.[57]

In fear of his life he passed his beautiful wife off as his sister whom Pharaoh then married. The Egyptian Gods disapproved of this liaison and punished the Pharaoh. When the truth of the matter was revealed he sent Sarah back to Abraham who then with his household was escorted to the Negev. In an astounding exhibition of generosity the Egyptians allowed Abraham to keep the wealth which he had accumulated.

Abraham, in this myth, credits not the Egyptians, but his personal exclusive God for his good fortune. This occurred in spite of his selfish anxiety and questionable behavior relative to his wife, Pharaoh, and the Egyptians. The evidence was convincing! His God was a God of unbounded love, limitless grace and unconditional mercy. No other God in the universe had these characteristics. Abraham's God was unique and special! Abraham could only conclude that he himself was therefore unique and special!

Abraham and his entourage returned to Palestine where they lived among the Canaanites and other tribal groups. These people had their own land, villages, cities and their own Gods. But Abraham, obsessed with the covenant, disregarded this reality.

He settled in a land which he claimed as his own. To make the claim was one thing. To make it a reality was quite another. The realization of the claim was conditioned on an expanded family, a powerful tribe or even an association of culturally cohesive tribes. But where was the evidence of his descendants who were to be as numerous as the stars of heavens. Where was the evidence of "God's People" who were to possess the land?[58] He had faith and conviction, nothing else. Among his numerous relatives and descendants, who would be chosen to occupy the land and become a mighty nation? It was evident that Lot, who had located his family in Sodom, was not in line for such honor.

The Selection Myths

Among all the peoples of the world some people are "God's people" and all others are not "God's people." This enduring segmentation of humanity was a deliberate and arbitrary act of Abraham's God. It became a doctrine enshrined and made sacred in the mythical covenant so absolutely crucial to the formation of the "children of Israel."

The selection of these "special people" is the second theme of the ancestral stories undergirding the theology of the "children of Israel." What is happening in these stories is a retrospective affirmation of a people's identity, significance and reason for being. They dramatically demonstrate the purpose of family stories and the fabrication of social history.

From the very beginning the continuity of special status and the fulfillment of the covenant was problematic.

Sarah is infertile. Abraham can do nothing.

But the God of Abraham impregnated Sarah.[59] Isaac is born. He is truly a son of God, a God-man. Thus he is selected as an appropriate symbol of "God's people," the "chosen people." Ishmael is the son of Abraham. He is not a son of God. He is not selected. His descendants are not chosen. He is banished to the wilderness and his people survive to be a great but alien people without promise.

The selection stories continue. No ordinary woman could be the mother of the next generation of selected people; certainly not the Canaanite women among whom they lived. God selected a relative of Abraham from the ancestral land of Chaldea, to be the wife of Isaac.[60]

But Rebekah is infertile. How can she be the mother of the descendants who shall be as numerous as the stars of the heavens? Abraham's God acted again and impregnated her.[61]

Twins, Jacob and Esau, are born. A selection is made. One will be the progenitor of "God's people" the other is notable only because he hunted, ate and drank and went his own way despising his brother and making life miserable for his parents.[62]

Isaac is significant in this myth because he reaffirmed the central thesis of the covenant. He replaces Abraham in a second version of the Abraham, Sarah and Pharaoh myth. The setting for this version is not Egypt but the Philistine community of Gerar. Rebekah is a beautiful woman. Isaac repeats the lies of his father with the same result.[63] He violates the moral standards of his benefactors but is enriched by those he had wronged. Surely proof again that his God has limitless unconditional mercy and blessings.

There is one final story in the selection of the progenitors of "God's chosen people." Jacob, the selected God-man, needs a wife. Again a local alien woman will not do. Jacob goes himself to the ancestral land. This land, as in the case of Rebekah, is something of a mystical, supernatural realm, an abode of sacred females, appropriate mothers of a special people.

Jacob returns with two wives. Numerous children are born to Leah and concubines. Rachel, the preferred wife is infertile. God impregnates her.[64] A God-man, Joseph, is born. The selective process is now complete. The progenitors of the "chosen people" are identified. They are the male descendants of the household of Jacob.

In these myths Sarah, Rebekah and Rachel, all remarkably beautiful women, have roles identical to those of Isis in Egyptian theology and the mother of Mithras in Persian theology. All of these women produced, as the consequence of God-induced pregnancies, special, select, unique God-men, carriers of special purposes, the hope of the future and saviors from human ills in both this life and the life to come.

It is in this latter function of God-men that Joseph comes to prominence.

The Salvation Myths

The world is a dangerous place for a unique, special and favored people. Can they survive all the physical and social threats of an alien and hostile world which cares neither for them or their exclusive singular God?

Joseph was a God-man who initiated a remarkable new phase in the myths of the Hebrew peoples. He was a son of God, born for a special purpose. He was born to be a savior of his people.[65] He is the first of many saviors and initiates a series of salvation myths.

This set of myths begins with a third version of the Abraham, Sarah and Pharaoh myth. Egypt again provides the setting.

There is again a famine from which the family must be saved. In addition there is the social condition of subservience from which God's "chosen people" must be rescued. Furthermore they must be saved from a multitude of sins and trials in the wilderness of darkness and death and finally saved to embark on their mission to save the world as the enlightened people in the Promised Land. The intervention of their God and his messengers, the God-men, take center stage in all these dramas.

At the beginning of this multifaceted salvation story is a family conflict. Joseph was the son of Jacob's favorite wife. Joseph was born because of a God-induced pregnancy, a God-man, a dreamer, an interpreter of dreams; perchance a spiritual man with unique access to the supernatural world. He has a coat of many colors! He is a God-man with many functions.

45

He was envied and hated by the sons of Jacob's other wife and concubines. They sold him into slavery and thus expelled him from the family and their life. Abraham thinks he was torn apart by beasts. In effect Joseph is dead and gone.

But some years later he reappears. He comes back into the life of the "chosen people" with a series of remarkable consequences. He rises to the highest level of social and political life in Egypt and is equivalent to the Pharaoh except for the throne. In Egypt the pharaohs are always sons of Ra the sun God, or sons of Osiris or their equivalents. They are God-men. They are reincarnations of Horus. Pharaoh recognized Joseph as an incarnation of the Gods, the Gods of Egypt.[66] Glory and honor are bestowed upon him. He has the power of a king and is something of a king among kings. The people of Egypt from the least to the greatest recognized him as a God-man and did obeisance.[67] A Horus parallel is inescapable.

This resurrection of Joseph, as the resurrection of every God-man, has a purpose. It demonstrates the power of life over death; this is the hope of salvation. He is resurrected in order to save his people. He saves them from starvation. He provides a renewal of life for the family. He saves the "chosen people" from social extinction. He creates a land of promise and prosperity, a social setting in an Egyptian paradise where they may become whole and healthy as a community and a people. He reestablishes intimacy with his brothers and enlightens their lives. He is a messenger from God. Above all and in summary he is a savior of his people.[68]

Egypt however is not the Promised Land. It is a land of leeks, onions and opportunity. It is not a land of spiritual well-being. It does not provide the setting for separation so desperately needed by a special, select and chosen people. They increased in numbers but their status decreased. Were

46

they still the "chosen people" of the God of Abraham, Isaac and Jacob or were they "slaves" enveloped by social darkness and approaching social death?

Was there some way they could be reconstituted as a special people? Was there some way in which their status as the "people of the God of Abraham, Isaac and Jacob" could be reestablished? Was there some way in which they could be resurrected and saved? Their myths pointed them to the only hope.

Moses, born of a Hebrew mother, was rescued from the waters, a symbol of turbulence but also a symbol of both death and life as in baptism. Moses, as Joseph before him was raised to the status of a pharaoh, a God-man.

The serpent, in the Moses version of the myth, initiates a third salvation myth. One facet of this myth reports that Moses' rod became a snake; a phenomenon which was repeated by the Egyptian seers, but Moses snake ate the Egyptian snakes.[69] The theme of their special status and the superiority of their singular God are reinforced. The uncertain world of the wilderness had manifold tribulations and threatening incidents. From all of these the ancestors had been saved. Their God, as he did in the classic plagues and struggle at the Red Sea, bested all adversaries.

In addition they experienced some new revelations. God was no longer simply and only the God of the ancestors, Abraham, Isaac and Jacob. He was now their God. He was the God of the wandering wilderness tribes who were saved and were now his "chosen people."

And he had a name. He was Jehovah (JHWH) (Yahweh), the Lord of Hosts, uniquely a God of war as well as the God of all things.

They made another discovery in the wilderness which was to haunt them for the rest of their days. Jehovah could become angry and could inflict punishment. This was not a part of the ancient covenant. An entire new chapter of relationship with their exclusive God now opened. The relationship became conditional.[70]

The people grumbled and God punished them with a plague of snakes. Moses, on God's instruction, raised a brass serpent on a pole. Those who gazed on this symbol were saved from death and restored to health.[71] We must recall that Hydra the serpent – a constellation adjacent to Taurus the bull in the celestial revelations – is an integral part of the tauroctony of Mithraism and is associated with the life-giving blood as it flows from the lethal wound inflicted by Mithras.

The commitment to trust their exclusive God in the geographical areas occupied by other Gods was more than many could bear. Their violation of the covenant took even the gross form of calf worship, a symbolic element in the worship of the local Gods. Perchance it was a male calf, a bull, one of the most remarkable symbols in the tauroctony and taurobolium of Mithraism, the religion of Abraham's ancestors in the Ur of Chaldea. These ancient ancestral commitments to the powers of the heavens, their astrological representations and the local Gods moved and motivated them when the going got rough.

But their own exclusive God was still there although they now related under a conditional covenant. They received another crucial revelation. Reconciliation with Yahweh could be accomplished by ceremonies of propitiation. This realization entered the Hebrew theological stream with remarkable consequences. The multiplication of sacrifices and ceremonial performance became central in their developing cultural identity.

Despite all these new insights, revelations and a modified covenant the original agreement of separateness and exclusion remained the ultimate and crucial condition. It was basic to their survival. They alone belonged to God. The rest of the human race was excluded.[72] This self-assessment, self-image and hope for domination stood at the core of Hebrew culture and theology. God remained a "great and terrible God"[73] to all other peoples. They alone had a way of reconciliation with him.

The final salvation myths involve the departure from the wilderness of trials, the crossing of the Jordon, entrance into the Promised Land, possession of the land and the development of a national state. All of this under the leadership of an explicit savior, Joshua.

The salvation from starvation, the salvation from Egypt, the salvation from the innumerable trials of the wilderness and the entrance into the "Promised Land" are the stories of salvation writ large. These myths informed the theology of an emerging people. Their God was a saving God. Their stories told them so. They were a covenant people, they were a selected people and they were a saved people. Their God in their myths had saved them in marvelous ways. He would save them again and again and ultimately fulfill the promises of the covenant in spite of their recalcitrance and niggardly cooperation.

The reaffirmation of myths is a critical social process in the formation of a "people" and these people had many myths to nourish their spiritual life and teach their children. To this end these stories were marvelous and reassuring.

Israelites: A People Struggling to Actualize their Myth

It is here where some semblance of history may begin. Who these people were and where they came from is something of a mystery. Sometime between the tenth and eighth centuries

BCE the ancestors of the Jews arrived in Palestine as family groups, even as extended family groups or tribes. They did have common myths, a common set of rituals and some sense of commonality and identity.

The tribes dispersed and found parcels of land among the native populations. They lived among many different peoples with many different Gods. They inevitably had contacts with these people, fraternized with them and intermarried. They even adopted aspects of their neighbors' culture. Given these realities how could the separateness and exclusion required by the original mythical covenant, be achieved.

The temptations to intermingle were ever present. The possibilities of contamination were fearsome. Their worship of Yahweh with its complex ceremonies, rituals and unique behavioral patterns were designed to establish social barriers.

There was never a moment in which they could escape their special status. The cyclical series of rituals from day to week to month to year reinforced internal social cohesion and reminded them of the covenant's exclusion requirement. It was inevitable that social contamination would occur. But there were always purification rites to restore them to favor with their jealous God.

Thus they lived in constant tension; a tension between the promises of their myths and the realities of their social existence.

Yahweh was still with them but he was now present in a holy book, a holy ark, a holy land and ultimately a holy temple which housed a Holy Spirit in whose presence they endeavored to become a holy people.

The myths were marvelous and exhilarating as long as one contemplated the promises. But the realities were quite different.

The Realities of Palestine

The children of Abraham, Isaac and Jacob never really occupied the land. They were forever interlopers among the native peoples. Their neighbors continued to worship their own Gods and Yahweh's people repeatedly violated the conditions of the covenant. They often found themselves in compromising moral and religious situations and even sought the help of neighboring local Gods.

The realization of nationhood, the acquisition of power and any contribution to the well-being of humanity was sporadic and minimally successful. Most of their history was spent in subjugation to tribal or national powers that had little regard for their God and no regard at all for the grand and glorious designs of their myths.

In the face of these realities they endured only as a minority group with a marvelous array of myths and a complex set of religious rituals. But, in spite of their social situation, they struggled to realize the grand design of the myths which they possessed and which possessed them.

In a summary way let us observe the following realities: These Israelites, these struggling peoples – a motley group of loosely related and affiliated tribes – arrived in Palestine sometime after 1000 BCE and occupied scattered segments of the land. These people with some elements of a common culture sought social identity and worked to establish social boundaries. Their myths were critical in the development of social cohesion. How else could they develop the integrity to form institutional structures necessary for social continuity?

They lived in a theistic world. The identification with the supernatural world provided a mystical union crucial to the struggle toward social identity. For these people it was a monstrous multifaceted struggle. A struggle with their God whose name they found confusing, a struggle with alien peoples, a struggle with the land and a struggle with the central myths underlying their very existence. They came to think of themselves as a people of struggle and hence their name Israelites, for Israel was their mythical founder who got his name in a spiritual, mythical struggle with God.

An endless struggle to make their myths into history ensued. The struggle centered on persuading their God to again act on their behalf.

The Conditional Covenant and Life

The covenant which seemed unconditional in its original version was modified by the myths of the exodus. The conditional nature of the covenant became a fundamental aspect of theological thought by the time the book of Nehemiah entered the stream of literary work.

As their society developed their God was still "the Lord God of heaven." He had always been the "great and terrible God" toward the enemies of his "chosen people." But he now "keeps covenant and steadfast love with those who love him and keep his commandments."[74] By implication he is now the great and terrible God to those who fail to love him and those who fail to keep his commandments even among the "chosen people."

But what does it mean to "love him?" This might be satisfied by the part of the covenant which specified their exclusive relationship with him, but was that enough. The keeping of his commandments was another matter. There were hundreds of commandments and rigorous ceremonies as described in the books of Exodus, Leviticus, Numbers and Deuteronomy.

Was there any way a human being could keep all these commandments?

And what were the consequences if violations occurred. What would their "great and terrible" God do?

By the testimony of their own priests and prophets, violations occurred. Serious violation such as worshipping other Gods, interrelating with alien peoples, becoming impure by failing to live up to innumerable commandments and failing even in the moral dimensions of the ten commandments.

Given these realities an extended coterie of religious functionaries were ordained to perform the intercessory activities for the people. Ceremonies, purification rituals and sacrifices were multiplied to placate their offended God. Blood sacrifices were the crux of the effort and in this they differed in no essentials from their neighbors.

They struggled to reestablish the purity of segregation. They struggled to fulfill their part in the mythological contract and thus entice their singular God to finally fulfill the ancient promises and actualize their superior status in this world. This was the controlling myth for the people. They were a struggling people. They were the children of Jacob who had struggled with God.[75] This is what made them Israelites.

In addition the abode of their God and the repository of their holy books were crucial to their hopes. The temple and associated activities were central to the survival of the myths, and their survival as a people. The expectations and hopes symbolized in these myths and implicit in the religious rituals and ceremonies is known as the "priestly tradition."

Messiah and the Priestly Tradition

At the core of this tradition was the awareness that crucial events in the stories of their origins were precipitated by God-men, messengers and saviors such as Abraham, Isaac, Jacob, Joseph, Moses and Joshua.

They had failed to possess the land. They had failed to become a powerful people. It was increasingly obvious that the realization of the promises could only be accomplished by another God-man, a Messiah. God would act, the Messiah would come and they would again be on the way to achieving the status which the God of their myths had promised.

But how was this event to be attained. They knew nothing more than the mechanisms of rituals, sacrifices and excruciating struggles to separate themselves from the contamination of surrounding cultures.

When they were pure the Messiah would come! By the last centuries BCE this theological doctrine was well developed and joined the other myths which sustained some segments of Jewish life and culture. The anxious, passionate and even frenetic ceremonies and sacrifices are understandable in this context.

For some Jews, the coming of the Messiah would inaugurate a political kingdom whose might and power the nations of the world would have to respect. This Messiah would be a king, even a king above all kings as their ancestral God was a God above all Gods. He might even be a military leader as the ancestral God Yahweh had been. The ancient promises would finally be realized in a real, powerful and prosperous national life.

As time went on and nothing changed, some segments of Jewish society began to question various aspects of these myths. They even dared to question the nature of the promises and the implication of their calling as a special people. Some began to question the nature of the blessings which they were supposed to receive and even the nature of Yahweh, their singular God. Some of their fundamental theological propositions were questioned.

In view of these doubts a second strain of theological constructs emerged. This school of thought is generally known as the "prophetic tradition."

The Prophetic Tradition, a National Moral Revival

Those in the prophetic tradition considered the moral degeneration of Jewish society as the central problem. But there was no agreement about a solution.[76]

From one perspective the Messiah, a messenger from God, would come and inspire a moral revolution. This Messiah would provide the power and techniques whereby Israel as a nation would become an example of morality and righteous living. They would thus become a blessing to all; indeed they would become a light to enlighten the whole world. This theme is present in the book of Isaiah.[77] It was a continuing theme among segments of Jewish society in Palestine and the Diaspora. But it is a theme with remarkable similarities to the function of Horus in Egyptian thought and Near Eastern versions of Mithras from Persian-Chaldean theology.

The Prophetic Tradition, an Ethical Way of Life for All Humans

The second perspective was a dramatic departure from traditional Hebrew theology.

In this perspective, there was a rejection of the nationalistic ideology. There was a rejection of the sacrificial rituals and religious ceremonies which were so central to the priestly tradition. Amos, an advocate of this view asked the question,

"With what shall I come before the Lord and bow myself before God on high? Shall I come before him with burnt offerings, with calves of a year old? Will the Lord be pleased with thousands of rams and ten thousand rivers of oil? Shall I give my firstborn for my transgression, the fruit of my body for the sin of my soul?"[78] The answer is a profound and resounding NO! Sacrifice as a way of serving God is out and, even more clearly, sacrifice as a solution for sin is forever rejected in the prophetic tradition.

But the Amos and Micah tradition have an additional dramatic message. "He has showed you, oh man, what is good and what does the Lord require of you but to do justice, and to love kindness and to walk humbly with your God."[79]

The people of God, according to these prophetic materials, are those people who reject exclusive status and all forms of sacrifice. All the notions of being a special people, in a special land, with a special political destiny are wiped away. What is left is a special quality of life. The people of God are those who live a life of justice, kindness, love and humility.[80] Thus the opportunity to be the people of God is open to all people.

This was the core idea of the prophetic message of Amos, Micah, Jonah and other writers who had taken the more radical second direction in prophetic tradition.[81] Some scholars would identify Jesus with this tradition.[82]

Myths and the First Century

Remnants and variations of the myths referred to throughout this chapter were part of Jewish culture. This was the theological world in which Jesus of Nazareth and Saul of Tarsus lived. This was one dimension of the theological world in which their followers were constructing a theology for their communities.

CHAPTER 5

THEOLOGY OF ASIA MINOR

The religious and theological dimensions of the culture of first century Asia Minor was a complex mix and amalgamation of the antecedent stories, myths and theologies from many sources. The most important of these were the myths and stories from Egyptian, Persian and Hebrew culture. It seems useful to summarize some of the crucial aspects of this culture in order to help us understand Jesus of Nazareth and his followers as well as Saul of Tarsus, his followers and the emergence of Christianity.[83]

Revelation from the Heavens

"In the beginning was God." This statement is a cultural universal. But "God" was always plural and variously named: Enneads, the Neteru, the Elohim, etc. These timeless powers were responsible for everything including the creation of other Gods.

The Gods created the sun, moon and stars and set them in order in the heavens. These heavenly bodies are not only the creation of the Gods but also represent the Gods and, from some perspectives, were considered to be Gods or spirits. In addition the Gods created the earth and everything including spirits and human beings.

These Gods and spirits have the capacity to interact with everything on earth including human beings. In turn human beings have access to them in various ways: direct conversation, meditation, prayer, rituals of sacrifice and ceremonies of worship, etc. The Gods have characteristics similar to human beings, consequently relationships between them are neither certain nor consistent.

The Gods may select certain people to be their own special protégés. Sometimes a contract between God and humans or human groups is established. Thus peoples of the first century had national Gods, local Gods and even family Gods. The relationship between people and Gods was generally conditional and could be revised by an arbitrary act of the deity.

It was possible for humans to offend the supernatural powers and thus incur a negative response. This could result in unpleasant physical or social conditions. Such consequences however could be ameliorated by returning to the good graces of the deities. The supernatural powers devised mechanisms and procedures whereby human beings could be forgiven and restored to favor with the Gods.

Crucial to the relationships between the supernatural world and human beings were the God-men. There were many God-men but all shared similar characteristics and functions. They demonstrated the consistency and the enduring concern of the Gods for human beings. They identified with the experiences of humans. They brought enlightenment, healing, wholeness and ultimate salvation.

These were general characteristics across broad reaches of the world of antiquity. But there were civilizations in which certain aspects were particularly prominent.

Elements from Egyptian theology

In Egyptian culture there was a particular emphasis on the role of the God-men at the point of transition from life in this world to life in the world of the Gods. The God-men came from the realm of the Gods and experienced life in its human aspects. They experienced death, dissolution or dismemberment at the hands of evil forces. However they were always rescued from the nether world or some form of distress or turbulence. They were reconstituted and resurrected.

Subsequently they returned to the supernatural world where they ushered people through death and guided them through the trials in the hall of judgment. Then as they stood or sat at the right hand of their father they acted as advocates as their human charges sought to become children of God.

Osiris and Horus in their repeated incarnations in the pharaohs of Egypt were remarkable God-men in all these aspects. They represented continuity and social stability. But their conflict with Seth symbolized the conflict of good and evil. Seth killed Horus/Osiris. Death and dissolution of these God-men seemed ultimately tragic and final. But the triumph of evil was short lived. The God-men were resurrected and reconstituted. New life emerged and hope revived.

These beliefs and associated rituals were present in the first and second century Roman world most explicitly in the cult of Cybil, the Roman version of Isis. The myths of this system of thought were elements of the worldview of the people of the Roman Empire and the Near East as Christianity was being formed.[84]

Elements from Persian-Chaldean Sources

Some special features from Persian Chaldean sources persisted in modified form and added to the mix of worldviews in the Near Eastern portions of the Empire. The worship of Mithra was practiced as early as the fourth century BCE in the Cilician region of modern day Turkey. It was officially sanctioned in some regions by the second century BCE.[85] By the beginning of our era it was a common philosophical and religious system in the Roman Empire.

Its central myth held that the powers of original creation still controlled all things; a fact demonstrated by the precession of the equinoxes. This certainty was celebrated in magnificent astrological cycles of the Ages of Taurus, Aries, Pisces and the coming Age of Aquarius.

This religious-philosophical system had great relevance to human life and experience. On the immediate social relational level there was the possibility of dying to the old, experiencing purification, and being reborn or experiencing a new regenerated life. The slaughter of the bull, the eating of the meat, the washing in the blood and the drinking of the blood symbolized these spiritual realities. Humans long for continuity, cleansing and rejuvenation. Participation in the Taurobolium ritual was a celebration of spiritual and emotional purification and rebirth.

But there was also an eternal significance to the Taurobolium ceremony. The concern about life, death and life beyond this world was and is persistent. Two thousand years ago the religion and philosophy of the Near East had answers for these ever-troubling questions.

Elements from Jewish theology

Another significant contributor to the mix of thought, particularly in the context where Jesus and Saul lived was the religious thought of the Israelites. This minority group historically wedged between the remnants of the ancient Egyptian and Persian Empires, had incorporated many theological ideas from its neighbors even as it struggled to establish a meaningful independent identity. To accomplish this end the Hebrews reformulated common myths of the region and added myths pertinent to their own social needs.

They identified and claimed a unique deity known first as "I am who I am" and later as Jehovah. As their name Israel implies, they struggled to become a "unique people" of a unique God. Their struggle was supported by myths of "covenant," "selection," "salvation" and "special purpose."

But, as things turned out, Jehovah's favors were very limited. Jehovah simply did not deliver the blessings their myths predicted. To this disappointment the people responded in different ways. Some simply gave up and scattered.

Some blamed themselves for having lost the favor of their God and in desperation struggled to reestablish good relationships with Jehovah. To this end they struggled to acquire purity by elaborate blood rituals, a practice common among their neighbors. It is hardly remarkable that the preferred animal for sacrifice was a lamb or goat. They lived in the age of Aries and not in the age of Taurus.

Behind all the struggles was the hope for the appearance of a new God-man, a new messenger from God, a Messiah who would fulfill the promises at the core of their controlling myths.

The Theology of antiquity is familiar

Most of what we have encountered in the first chapters of this book is familiar to Christians. There are very few new ideas in our world. Thoughts, ideas, religious dogmas and understandings of the supernatural have been common properties of the human race since very early times. Christianity has modified the referents but we can still recognize the fundamental motifs. An appreciation of the similarities and continuities can be an enriching experience.

The theological elements discussed in the early chapters of this book are by no means exhaustive. Many others would be important to an understanding of the formation of Christianity. Others would be important to later developments as the church added and emphasized elements which were not important in the earlier days of Christianity. One of these is the symbol form often referred to as a cross.

The Cross in Antiquity

The symbol of the cross is one of the more universal symbols. The form varies across cultures and even within cultures. But regardless of the form it seems to have a general meaning. But what does it symbolize. To what fundamental aspect of human life and experience does it point?

The forms of the cross in the ancient world were manifold. A common one was simply the form we call X. The earliest Egyptian form was T shaped. A significant variation had the vertical shaft of the T extend upwards. This variation became known as the Roman Cross. A common variation of the Egyptian cross has an oval or ring-shaped top with the oval form extending below the crux of the cross.

The cross appears in association with pictorial representation of many myths. The Egyptian Madonna scene, featuring Isis with Horus on her lap, has an Egyptian cross on the back of her chair. Osiris, in his role as God of the dead, is pictured extending this cross to dying humans. The Egyptian priests wore a cloak with the vertical shaft of the cross embroidered on the front and back and the horizontal shaft on the sleeves. The virgins devoted to the adoration of the Roman Goddess Vesta wore a cross as a pendant.

In the Persian and Babylonian civilizations the cross appears in various forms. The Sun God Bel or Baal had a cross as their symbol. Kings of those ancient kingdoms wore crosses in the shapes we now associate with the Maltese cross and St Andrews cross.

The cross itself was often embellished with other symbols attached to the crux. One of the most common was the symbol of the sun. This complex symbol was common in early churches and is still present in stained glass windows in some Christian churches today.[86] In the millennia BCE the cross often had a lamb mounted at the crux and this symbol also still appears in some Christian settings.

In addition to these rather rigid forms the sign of the cross was used in various ceremonial and celebrative settings. In Egypt the cross was used as a ritual marking on celebrants in religious ceremonies. The T cross was marked on the foreheads of initiates into Mithraism. Egyptians marked their sacred cakes with a cross. Some commentators are convinced that the mark placed on the head of the righteous (Ezekiel 9:4) was a T.

The evidence is overwhelming. The cross was widely represented in all the pre-Christian civilizations of the Near East and Rome. But what did it symbolize?

Certainly at its core was an understanding of the intersection of the light and heat from the sun intersecting with the earth to produce life. The Sun God and the Earth Goddess combine to produce life. It is no accident that one of the most common complex symbols of the cross had the emblazoned sun at its crux. Ancient peoples were not afraid of sexuality or fertility symbols to express some of the deepest insights into the meaning of existence.

The cross in ancient myths is associated with life, light and enlightenment. Osiris, in his role as God of the dead extends a cross to the dying person as a sign of resurrection and hope for the new life in the eternal spiritual world. The sword in some tauroctony depictions is a T shaped cross in the hands of the God-man Mithras as the blood flows to regenerate life on the earth and from the earth.

The cross, for the people of the ancient world, symbolized the dynamic interaction between the powers of the heavens and all the elements of the earth. In a summary way it demonstrated the intersection of the power of the sun God with mother earth. It is the icon of the generation of new life and hope in every new day, every new year, every new age, every new eon, and every new life. Death is never the end – it is simply a transition to life, even a more meaningful life. Life and new life lies deep in the crux of the cross. It did in antiquity and it does to this day.

Theology and Life in the Near East

A complex amalgamation of myths, symbols and religious ideas from Egyptian, Persian, Jewish, Greco-Roman and other sources provided the theological and philosophical thought structure of the people in the Near East in the first centuries CE. It was this complex of ideas which informed the mind and spirit of the gentile world and the Jewish Diaspora. This corpus of religious material was used by Paul and succeeding generations of theologians as they formulated the doctrines of Christianity.

Academia at the Turn of Our Era

It should be observed that the myths and stories alluded to in the preceding materials were not the only thought structures of the Greco-Roman world. The philosophical ruminations of Plato and Socrates, the scientific thought of Hipparchus, the mathematical genius of Pythagoras appealed to many. Remarkable schools of learning existed.

An accumulation of centuries of learning in mathematics, medicine, geometry, geography, astronomy, literature, history, philosophy, rhetoric, drama and other disciplines existed. Libraries with many thousands of scrolls and codices existed in Alexandria, Athens, Rome and other centers of learning. Even the Celtic civilizations of central Europe had universities with extensive libraries and many students.

These scholars had different concerns and viewed the world in ways quite different than the masses of the people. These intellectuals and their learning were a factor in the culture of the early centuries of our era.

Meaning and the Common Man

But the masses of people, most of them illiterate, were engaged in the grim realities of survival and had little contact with the knowledge of the scholars. They viewed the world through the screen of meaning provided by their ancient myths. The average man toiling in the fields, the village craft shops and the cities of the Near East, when asked to describe his understanding of the universe and his place in it, would have responded with these stories. These myths were as ageless as time and as new as the next dawn. They were the source of spiritual sustenance. They provided the context in which life was tolerable. These myths held the key to the meaning of human existence and the meaning of the supernatural world with which they were ultimately engaged.

Thus there existed in the first centuries of the CE a vast reservoir of myths and symbols. As change occurred some of these were applied directly to the evolving social world, others were modified and produced new thoughts and practices. Still others were misapplied and became radically distorted with devastating consequences.

Myths, Choice and Consequences

The people of antiquity, Jesus and Saul in their day and we ourselves in our day are preserved or destroyed by life-controlling myths.

Jesus and his followers essentially rejected the popular theologies of his day. They paid little attention to myths, doctrines and dogmas. They advocated a life of love and its application to all human relationships. In another context I have described this as "Jesus Christianity."[87]

Saul found the myths of Asia Minor to be the context in which he understood Jesus and his own world. This worldview planted the seeds which, by the fourth century produced Constantinian Christianity."[88] This kind of Christianity emerged because it reinstituted, reformulated, literalized and historicized the essential features of the complex amalgam of Persian, Egyptian, and Hebrew theological thought which had coalesced in Asia Minor. It was the kind of Christianity which emphasized a literal understanding of Jesus Christ, fidelity to creeds and an hierarchical order of church administration. It was the kind of Christianity which came to full bloom in the medieval period and is still the main core of both Protestant and Catholic Christianity. It is to these phenomena we now turn.

CHAPTER 6

THE DAMASCUS ROAD CONVERSION

The followers of Jesus were often confused about Jesus' work and purposes while he lived. His death added to the uncertainty. By the time a generation had passed, the "Jesus movement" was already a fragmented community with diverse interpretations and practices.

Saul of Tarsus, two decades after the death of Jesus became an important figure in the interpretation of Jesus and his work. Paul's (Saul's) missionary endeavors and letters further compounded the confusion and contributed to an enduring division. His interpretation of Jesus made an accommodation to critical elements in the religious thought and dogma of both the Jewish Diaspora and the gentile religious culture of Asia Minor. From the most crucial perspectives Saul's interpretation and doctrinal formulations about Jesus bore little resemblance to the work of the itinerant teacher and preacher of the previous generation.

Saul, according to his own testimony, never met Jesus in person. At best he had oral reports about Jesus and apparently knew little about his teachings, parables, aphorisms and down-to-earth stories about the way to live with one's fellowmen. He did know about Jesus as a troublemaker. He knew that Jesus had taught ideas and advocated principles which threatened the Jewish religious leaders and the local Roman authorities. He knew that Jesus had been convicted of sedition and heresy. He knew about the crucifixion but probably little more.

But Saul did know about the followers of Jesus. He knew they were continuing to live and teach the principles of life which Jesus had taught. He knew these principles of life and relationships were a threat to Jewish religious doctrines. He knew the social doctrines which they advocated were at variance with the hierarchical principles on which Roman society was built. Everything about the followers of Jesus challenged his worldview. They threatened his religious commitments and they threatened his security as a citizen in the Roman Empire. They were a menace to religious orthodoxy and social stability. He feared and hated them with a fury.[89]

While on the road to Damascus, intent on persecuting the followers of Jesus, Saul had a remarkable experience. He claims to have met Jesus in some spiritual way.[90] This experience changed his life. What was the nature of this phenomenon? What was this event which is sometimes described as Saul's conversion to Christianity?

Some have speculated at length about the psychological turmoil which a hate-filled mind endures as it goes about the task of destroying those it fears. Was this event the culmination of years of anger and hostility? Was it an emotional and psychological event designed to resolve the inner turmoil which was making life impossible for Saul? Or was it something much more profound with cosmic dimensions? Is it possible we can understand this event only if we understand the social world in which Saul lived?

The Worldview of Saul of Tarsus

The Greco-Roman civilization stood large and late among the civilizations which gave rise to our own. It was a civilization with a philosophical and religious system which had been influenced by manifold extensions of Egyptian and Persian thought. Myths from these sources migrated through centuries into Europe and the Near East. Here they amalgamated with local religious and philosophical ideas and produced a complex worldview.

By the time Rome displaced Greece as the dominant power, the common religious beliefs were amalgamations and variations of the ancient myths discussed in the preceding chapters. The region where Jesus and Saul lived was one of the most remarkably diverse parts of the Roman Empire. It was home to many ethic groups, with various religious persuasions.

As early as 390 BCE a western version of Mithraism was present in Tarsus. Some four centuries later when Saul was in his formative years Mithraism was the cutting edge of religious thought and was emerging as a controlling ideological system among the Roman legions, some intellectual elites, and the politically powerful administrators of the Roman provinces of Asia Minor.

The dogmas and symbols of this religious system were significant; but there was also an extensive moral code embedded in its philosophy. Absolute respect for authority, obedience, loyalty, integrity and asceticism were essential elements and celibacy was considered desirable. The application of these behavioral characteristics to personal, interpersonal and social relationships provided the basis for stable institutions and an enduring society.

Saul was an intellectual. He was also a religiously sensitive man. As an educated person he was engaged with the thought and ruminations of his friends and associates in the schools of Tarsus. He knew the theology, the astrology and the scriptures of mythology.[91] These were the materials of philosophical and literary interest and the subject of discussion and debate.

But he was also a Jew of the Diaspora. He had spent time in Jerusalem studying with the leading minds of pharisaic

Judaism. He was acquainted with the Old Testament and other materials crucial to the formation of Jewish thought.

It must be observed that every human being has been shaped by their socialization. Saul's view of the world was formed and fixed in the overlap, integration and fusion of Jewish thought and the culture of the Greco-Roman world.[92] It was in this kind of milieu he spent his youth, was educated and grew to maturity. It provided the screen of meaning which enabled him to make sense of the world in which he lived.

As an intellectual with a philosophical bent, he was keenly aware that military might, in the long run, could not produce the cohesion necessary for an enduring society nor provide security for minority groups of which he was a part. He was aware that social stability depended on the value structures underlying society. Social order depended on a general consensus concerning the nature of reality and the duties of all in the interests of the common good. Social order ultimately depends on the sacralization of the social system. The Greco-Roman versions of Egyptian mythology and the myths of Mithraism with its moral system performed this function.

At the turn of our era Roman domination of the Near East, North Africa and Europe had produced Pax Romana. There were pockets of social unrest.[93] But in general the Roman Legions controlled vast areas and imposed relative peace.

The genius of the Roman Empire was the hierarchical organization of all its institutions. There was a ranking of roles, a ranking of worth, and a ranking of responsibility in all aspects of society. For example: in the family institution the father was higher in rank than the mother, males were higher in rank than females, and the older ranked higher than the younger. In the political institution rank ordering from highest to lowest was: emperor, senator, citizen, non-citizen and, at the bottom, slave.

These social patterns were undergirded by religious and philosophical morality and sacralized in the ritualistic ceremonies of the Empire. The elite and the powerful found these principles remarkably effective in the maintenance of social order. Every person in the system knew his place and behaved accordingly. The masses of people kept their place out of respect for the system or habit or fear.

Saul of Tarsus was an intellectual, thoroughly acquainted with the philosophical and religious underpinnings of the societies of the region. He thought about these things. He knew and appreciated the moral code of the culture and had made this disciplined way of life his own. He was a Jew but he was a Roman Jew who had made peace with the world and culture in which he lived. He knew intimately both systems of thought and their overlapping values. He had arrived at a synthesis of these social realities and was intellectually and emotionally committed to them.

Into his world intruded a new and disquieting Jewish religious sect, the "Jesus followers."

The Worldview of the Followers of Jesus

These "followers of Jesus" proposed an alternate definition of both this and the supernatural world. This group of people called into question the central religious dogmas of both the Jewish and Greco-Roman world. Most particularly they called into question the ethics and morals relative to the nature of inter-human relationships.

Jesus and his followers advocated practical down to earth ways for humans to relate to one another. Jesus had called people to a new life; a life out of the mainstream of religious expectations. This life was not based on supernatural spirits and Gods. Neither was it based on the principles of hierarchical interpersonal relationships or the strictures of religious purity.[94]

Jesus' kind of life replaced rigid discipline with a remarkably different kind of human relationship. It replaced hierarchical social structures with a commitment to human social equality. It replaced control by law and fear with redemptive relationships of compassion, caring, acceptance and forgiveness. It replaced the exclusive nature of religious righteousness and social class with a call for all humans to grow toward a practical sense of equality and oneness.

It repudiated the selfishness of individualism and competition and called people to see others as they saw themselves. It called all men to a sharing of all aspects of life on the deepest levels. It sought to eliminate the advantage of wealth and power. It called all to escape the crippling effects of envy, hatred and fear. It placed love at the core of all relationships including all relationships with fellow humans and the very earth itself.

For the "followers of Jesus" this was the way to become human in the fullest sense; to escape the controlling cycles imposed by the spirits and Gods of the supernatural world. It was the only way to escape the degrading consequences of a hierarchical social structure. Jesus' message was a call for all men and women to escape individualism. He called all humanity to join the human race and escape the dehumanizing consequences of isolation and exclusion.

Fundamental Problems for Saul of Tarsus

It was clear to Saul that the culture of the "followers of Jesus" and the Greco-Roman-Jewish culture were antithetical at the deepest level. He could see no point of reconciliation. He feared a breakdown of religion and morality and a subsequent dissolution of the very structures of society if the "Jesus way of life" became common.

In this context the intensity of his persecution of the "followers of Jesus" is understandable.

He had spent years thinking about this group, fearing and hating it. With the best of intentions he was persecuting it and hoping to restore its people to what he thought was true religion, true morality, and thus ensure social stability.

But there were problems! There were contradictions! Things were not as clear as Saul wanted them to be. How could these people live a life of compassion and fearlessness in the face of persecution?

Saul had to recognize that the way of life of the "Jesus followers" was unusually humane if not holy. Even the most devout of his compatriots did not exhibit such down-to-earth concern for their fellowmen or such a composed and tranquil way of life. How could these people continue to have such loyalty to a peasant teacher who had been rejected by the learned leaders of the true religion and had been executed as a troublemaker and seditionist by the Roman authorities? How was this possible?

What dynamic lay at the core of the life of these people?

Saul could not escape the fact that for a particular and unique group of people Jesus was a remarkable person. Saul knew little of this Jesus of Nazareth. But he could not escape the fact that this Jesus was, for those who followed him, a great man, a giant of a man, a man of renown.[95]

Saul had to admit that this Jesus was a marvelous leader. In a few short years of teaching, preaching and interacting with people of all kinds he had gathered a following, including disciples who companied with him on a regular basis. He had preached doctrines and ethics which inspired the positive interest of multitudes. Obviously he was a hero to his followers. And even more; it was obvious that Jesus was a man whose doctrines and ethics were sufficiently dynamic to provide the courage for martyrdom.

Faced with these realities Saul could not dismiss Jesus lightly. As a matter of fact he could not dismiss him at all!

It became clear to Saul that Jesus was a great man, a giant of a man, who plumbed the depths of the human condition and provided answers for the real problems of human existance. But it was this very message and the following Jesus generated that made him a dangerous man.

But was Jesus really a dangerous man? Was his way of life actually a threat to the social order? The questions would not go away!

It was these dilemmas which troubled Saul's mind and roiled his spirit as he traveled the road to Damascus.

Great men before had been killed. Men with messages from the supernatural world had been rejected. Even God-men, the very revelations from the supernatural world, had not been recognized. Saul knew that God-men had been reviled, tortured and killed, only to be resurrected.

Was it possible that he was mistaken about this Jesus? Was it possible that this peasant storyteller and preacher of a universal ethical way of life was a God-man? Could he be a new messenger, could he be a Messiah, could he be a new Christ, a new incarnation of Horus or Mithra or Moses?

Could it be?

Was it really possible that this Jesus was a new God-man?

Saul Converted Jesus into a Christ

And then he was struck with the blinding light of the cosmic truth.

It had to be true! Jesus was a God-man!

Jesus was the messenger for whom his people had waited. Jesus was the avatar, the Christ for whom the religions of the region waited at the beginning of the new age.

Suddenly, for Saul, Jesus was a Christ, the current incarnation of the avatars of the past. He was the modern day representative from the supernatural world, as Mithra had been two thousand years before and as Horus had been many centuries earlier. He was the Messiah for his own ethnic community. He was a new Christ for the gentile world. It was an astounding thought! It was a terrifying thought. It was a most marvelous and overpowering revelation, an insight sufficient to shatter all his securities and humble all his preconceptions.

The cosmic light had come and struck him down!

Very little of Saul's worldview had to change. The only thing that changed was his classification of Jesus. Saul, in his revised system of belief, moved Jesus from the category of "man and troublemaker" into the category of "God-man." Jesus, whom he had despised, feared and hated, he now believed to be a new Christ. And this new Christ had all the characteristics of the Christs of antiquity.

Paul's Mission and Message

As Saul came to terms conceptually and emotionally with this realization his task in life became clear. He was a new man with a new purpose. His new conviction was the profound old message of the ages. He was driven by the excitement of cosmic connections and his own part in this cosmic drama.

He had a message to share with his Jewish and gentile compatriots. These people knew something of God-men, messengers, messiahs, avatars, Christs and saviors of the ages. Now Saul had a new version, a modern adaptation, a current and relevant understanding of the ancient myths. This Jesus, whose followers he had feared, was actually a God-man, a new messenger. Saul came to believe that Jesus should really be described as a Christ. So the name of Jesus became "Christ Jesus" or "Jesus Christ."

For Saul, this insight was life changing. It was so remarkable that he perceived himself to be a different man and changed his name to Paul. It was a revelation which had to be shared. He set out to bring this good news, this gospel, to any who would hear.

Paul committed his life to teaching and preaching about this new Christ. He was convinced that his fellow Jews and gentile compatriots in Asia Minor, Palestine and Europe would listen. He would introduce them to this new God-man, this Messiah, this Christ, this contemporary supernatural messenger for the new age.

As he preached this doctrine he characterized this new Christ with the old and ancient descriptive terms: "Son of God," "light of the world," "Lord," "King," "Master," "Savior," "redeemer," "advocate," "bringer of light and enlightenment" and many more terms which had been applied to the Christs of antiquity

For Paul this Jesus Christ was surely at the pinnacle of the hierarchical structure of the supernatural world in this new age. Surely this new Christ would fulfill the roles which previous Christs had performed. Surely he would be a savior and a rejuvenator of humans. Ultimately he would take his place at the right hand of his father and be an advocate for all men as they sought to become sons and daughters of God in the great, eternal supernatural world. This Christ, like other Christs of antiquity, would intervene and save his human people.

As he preached this doctrine he also reminded his hearers of their traditional morality. To this message he would add crucial elements which seemed to be trademarks of Jesus the new Christ. Jesus' ethic, expressed in behaviors such as love, joy, peace, patience, kindness, goodness, faithfulness, gentleness and self-control, was incorporated into Paul's traditional moral code and became an element in his instructions to the churches.[96]

The astrological age of Pisces had just arrived. Paul was convinced that this new Christ could serve as the electrifying component in a revision of religious thought in the early years of this new age.

Paul attempted to company with the earlier followers of Jesus. But there were differences of understandings about Jesus and these became insurmountable barriers. He went his own way.[97] Although he had never companied with Jesus he still claimed to be an apostle, even a superior apostle. He prided himself in being a special apostle, an apostle to the gentiles.[98] This division was never healed.

His interpretation of Jesus found a hearing among some Jews. But it was among the gentiles where he had his greatest success. In this social milieu the myths of antiquity were better known. The Christ characteristics which Paul preached were not strange. The converts to his doctrines and the churches which he founded became followers of his particular version of Jesus Christ.

Jesus and Paul: Irreconcilable Differences

The followers of Jesus had a different orientation. They sought to follow the way of life which Jesus had taught and demonstrated. They lived a life of compassion. They continued to follow a marvelous teacher and preacher, a human being whose loving and forgiving ways had brought healing and wholeness to their spirits and souls. They, like

Jesus, were primarily concerned about the way to live with their fellow men. These followers of Jesus had little concern for the Gods and the God-men of the supernatural world. They found little of value or relevance in the myths of antiquity. They were a community of human beings who cared about one another in this world just as Jesus, the man, had cared for them when he was alive.

Paul, in sharp contrast, was primarily concerned with the supernatural world, its God-men and their intrusion and functions in this world. In particular he was immersed in and controlled by his conviction that Jesus was a God-man, a Christ.[99]

Jesus followers perceived Jesus as a man of love and reconciliation. Paul saw Jesus as a supernatural God-man. These doctrines were worlds apart. They are as far apart as this known world is from the unknown supernatural world; probably an infinite distance.

From these radically different interpretations of Jesus two remarkably distinct streams of thought and life emerged. One stream concentrates on the supernatural world and its workings. The other strives to follow Jesus and engage in the kind of human relationships which Jesus taught and practiced; the kind of relationships which really redeem and make human beings healthy and whole.

The struggle between these streams of Christianity had remarkable consequences in the early centuries of our era. An assessment of the events of those struggles will provide an explanation of the dilemmas which plagued the medieval world and which still plague our world today. The next chapters will make an introduction to this subject.

CHAPTER 7

JESUS CHRIST IN THE NEW TESTAMENT

Paul succeeded in identifying Jesus with the Christs of antiquity. He spent the rest of his life preaching about this Christ. People who believed his doctrines were called Christians and they formed churches. Paul wrote letters attempting to clarify his doctrines and connected this message to a mix of his traditional morality and the ethics which he learned from the followers of Jesus.

The letters of Paul which appear in the New Testament have many references to "Jesus Christ." The descriptive names and functions ascribed to "Jesus Christ" are neither new nor unique. Most if not all had been applied to the "messengers." "the anointed ones" the "Christs" of antiquity. The theologies of the civilizations BCE had elaborated all these characteristics in a most comprehensive way.

Paul's Christ in the New Testament

Paul's description of "Jesus Christ" in the New Testament is parallel to the characteristics of the Christs of antiquity. The following paragraphs summarize some of the names and functions which are common to the Christs of antiquity and the Jesus Christ of Paul.

Paul in his missionary endeavors in Antioch spoke about the "son of God" using a quotation from the Psalms but with obvious reference to Jesus Christ. He also refers to Jesus Christ as God's "begotten" (Acts 13:33). As a son of God, Jesus Christ is logically and consistently, with other Christs, a "King" and "Lord" (Ephesians 1:17).

Jesus Christ in spite of being a "son of God" was also a "son of man." He was in human form as other Christs had been (Philippians 2:8-11). He was a God-man. This characterization is one of the most common genealogical designations of the ancient Christs of whom Horus and Mithras are excellent examples.

Jesus Christ brings enlightenment, dispels darkness and enables a life in association with the supernatural (Ephesus 4:17-18).

He is a redeemer. This is ordinarily understood to refer to a process of renewal and rebirth in the cycles of existence when one is faced with devastating consequences of failure. (Titus 2:14). It is this reality which lies at the core of the Mithras myth. It is ceremonially dramatized in the Taurobolium and pictorially portrayed in the Tauroctony. The renewal for humans occurs in a spiritual rebirth in the context of identification with the Christ's death and resurrection (Ephesians 4:8-9). The myths of Osiris, Horus and Mithras make this point.

Redemption occurs in the context of conflict. In all the examples from antiquity the powers of evil are unleashed and the son of God, the God-man, is abandoned by the heavenly powers (Romans 8:32). Evil powers triumph whether it is Seth, Satan, Judas Iscariot, the Romans or non-comprehending religious functionaries. Consequently the Christs experience death. Death is followed by descent into Hades, dismemberment, scattering to unknown places or the symbolic turbulence of the timeless seas.

But these defeats and degradations are only temporary. The Enneads or Elohim or Gods or their incarnations always come to the rescue of the God-men and restore them to life. Even Isis, a female deity in Egyptian theology, or Ishtar in Greek mythology performed this function in the rescue and reconstitution of their God-men husbands. This is the central theme of the Christs as they represent the life, death, resurrection, new birth and new life cycle.

The Christs after their sojourn, death and resurrection in this world go to the supernatural world. In that world they are raised to powerful positions and are found to be standing or sitting at the right hand of an accepting superior God often referred to as "father" (Ephesians 1:20, Romans 8:32).

The phenomenon of redemption for humans occurs in the fullest sense when they are ushered into the supernatural world. Here the humans experience judgment and then are presented by the Christ to his father.

Here the Christ's role as "mediator" (1 Timothy 2:5) or "intercessor" (Romans 8:34) is a dynamic symbol of the beneficence of the Gods. The Gods have provided care for humans on earth but more significantly they advocate and facilitate a permanent fellowship with the supernatural powers (Romans 8:27-36). Whether the Christ is Horus or Jesus and the father is Osiris, Ra or Jesus' father in Heaven, the lesson and its import are identical.

I invite you to peruse Paul's materials further and compare them with the literature related to Christs of antiquity indicated in the earlier chapters. It is hardly a coincidence that the theological ideas and the vocabulary are identical.

The influence of Paul on the non-Pauline New Testament materials

But what of scriptures in the New Testament which are not attributed to Paul? There are 12 of these documents. None of these were written, at least in final form, until decades after Paul had established churches and written his letters. We have none of the original documents. The versions we have in the New Testament were modified as they were written, re-written and copied through the second and third centuries.

Through this period of time Paul's particular theological views had circulated through the churches. These doctrines had time to mature, crystallize and spread. They had been discussed and finally absorbed into the general thinking of the early Christians. The names, characteristics and functions of the Christs which Paul had imposed on Jesus were widely accepted in the churches as standard theology. Thus the materials written in the decades after Paul were written by people who had been indoctrinated with Paul's theological conceptions.

This is true of the late materials attributed to Mathew and Mark. It is true of Luke who was a gentile follower of Paul. It is certainly true of the most explicit theological work of the New Testament, the document we know as the "Gospel of John." It is not surprising then that Jesus Christ in these materials is characterized explicitly and unambiguously in the mold of Paul's understanding of the Christs of antiquity.

With this brief description of the production of the non-Pauline materials in the New Testament let us turn to the characterizations of Jesus Christ which we find there.

Christ characteristics in non-Pauline New Testament materials

The prologue to the Gospel of John reiterates the fundamental proposition of all the Christs of antiquity "In the beginning was the word and the word was with God and the word was God" (John 1;1). Christians generally identify "word" with Jesus Christ. It is even explained at times as "message." Jesus Christ is then a "messenger." In this non-Pauline document he is again identified as God. Jesus Christ like all the other Christs was with God from the beginning (John 1:2). He like other Gods was a creator, even a creator of all things (John 1:3-10) which identifies him with the supreme Gods, the Enneads of Egyptian, Chaldean and Persian theology who created the Gods who created the universe.

In the book of Revelations, Jesus Christ is declared to be timeless and all encompassing; "I am the Alpha and Omega, the first and the last, the beginning and the end" (Rev. 22:13).

Jesus Christ like all other Christs is "life" and "light." This "life" and "light" is the source of life and light or enlightenment for all humans in this world. It is the kind of light which darkness could not overcome (John 1:5,9) just as the evil darkness of Seth could not, in the final analysis, overcome the light and life of Osiris and Horus.

Jesus Christ like all other Christs ultimately provides humans with the opportunity for birth into the supernatural world where they may become sons of God (John 1:14)

John declares Jesus Christ to be a God-man with the characteristics of "grace," "truth" and "glory" (John 1:15). These assertions would be at home in the funnery rites of ancient Egyptians as the devotees of Ra, Osiris and Horus intoned prayers to their deities.

The prologue of the gospel of John is a marvelous summary of the core theological ideas of the ancient world. The inclusion of this material in the writings of John many decades after the work of Saul of Tarsus illustrates the extent to which the theologies of the Christs had permeated the Church. The inclusion of these scriptures in the New Testament in the fourth century indicates the extent to which the bishops of the church had accepted Jesus as a God-man with all the characteristics of the Christs of Antiquity.

Jesus the Christ is described as "Immanuel" which is generally translated "God with us" (Mathew 1:23). Messengers are sent into this world by God (John 3:19) and are representatives of the Father. Horus, the son of Osiris was a "God with us" in all his incarnations in the theology of the Egyptians. The gospels describe Jesus Christ in this role in a most explicit way. He was the Messiah, a messenger from God.

The nature of the message is multifold. It provides enlightenment (John 8:12), salvation (John 3:19) and life (John 3:16).

But life is a phase in the ongoing sequence and cycle of death and life. Life in Christian theology, as in the theologies of antiquity, is inevitably the outcome of death and resurrection. The death of Horus, his dismemberment, and reconstitution symbolize the reality that death precedes new life. This is also the central message of Persian theology which had enduring impact through Mithraism.

Jesus Christ is the central figure in the Christian version of this profound myth. Central to the gospel in Christianity is the declaration "I am the resurrection and the life" (John 11:25).

But in order for new life to emerge; even eternal and never ending life, there must be death. Death is absolutely preliminary to new birth and new life. This profound truth is explicitly at the core of the gospels of the New Testament as it was in the writings of Paul and as it was in the myths of antiquity. This function of Jesus Christ is summarized in a remarkable passage (Mark 8:31). "He then began to teach them that the Son of Man must suffer many things and be rejected by the elders, chief priests and teachers of the law, and that he must be killed and after three days rise again". The New Testament scriptures are very clear; "the son of man…must be killed" an event preliminary to "rising again."

Frequently the terms salvation and redemption occur in relation to this two-sided sequence. The first part of the sequence is a condition that is bad, painful, destructive and evil, in Christian terms "sinful." But this is not necessarily a permanent condition. One can be saved. The transition from being "unsaved" to being saved requires a death and a resurrection. A death to the old followed by a birth to the new. This new life is a life cleansed from all the dross of the preceding sinful condition.

All the relevant myths and rituals of antiquity reminded humans of this basic reality. It is a reality which has provided hope for all peoples since the beginning of time. Jesus Christ was another Christ at the core of this enduring myth.

This central story of the New Testament is expressed in the Christian Eucharist.[100] This festival centers on the eating of the flesh and drinking of the blood of Christ. It is an exact parallel to the Taurobolium as it was practiced at the turn of our era. In that ceremony the death of the bull at the hands of the God-man Mithras, marked the end of an age and the beginning of a new age. Both are festivals of participation in the cycle of death and rebirth. They symbolize the death of old ways of living and the birth of new ways of living.

Blood was spilt in both cases and with the same purpose. The ceremonial feasting on the body of the sacrifice and the drinking of the blood takes the celebrant to the core of the intent of the Gods to bring new life. This communion ceremony is the crucial statement of the life-changing possibility for humans as they understand and identify with the cyclical nature of the universe. Participation represents a death to the old, a cleansing, purification and resurrection to new life.

Communion is a celebration of access to spiritual and moral health and new beginnings at crucial moments in life. It is a ceremony anticipating the ultimate resurrection to new life with the Gods, as understood by the Egyptians thousands of years earlier. It is an ancient ritual whose meaning has remained constant for thousands of year in many cultures.

All the preceding New Testament references are familiar to Christians. Their meanings were already familiar to the general culture of the Near East and Egypt centuries before Jesus was crucified in Palestine.

Where is Jesus in the New Testament?

Given these social realities we probably should be surprised that anything of Jesus, the man, and his ethical teachings appear in our records of the early church. The task of uncovering the intimations and hints of Jesus and his message is indeed challenging. But these hints and intimations do exist as underlying currents and probably appear most explicitly in the stories and parables attributed to Jesus. But in this mix of Christ and Jesus materials in the New Testament, confusion is almost inevitable. We must search in the profound difference between Jesus and the Christs to find faith in the Jesus way of life.

CHAPTER 8

JESUS CHRIST THE ONLY CHRIST

Theologically there is very little new in the New Testament. Christs had been known for centuries. Death and resurrection were central motifs in the "messenger" myths of antiquity. The meaning of these myths underlay the life of multitudes of people in various cultures through vast spans of time.

Christianity absorbed the crucial element of these myths. But what these elements meant in the modern world was confusing. Controversy appeared in the theology of the church from the very beginning. The Jesus Christ of Paul was interpreted in different ways and as time went on the confusion was compounded. The social impact of these controversies has been profound. The 21st century shows no signs of resolving the issues.

At the root of the problem is the assumption and belief that **Jesus**, the **Jesus Christ** of Paul and **Jesus the Christ** of fourth century Christianity were one and the same. I have hypothesized that these are three distinct and separate entities. They are remarkably different intellectual constructs. They are three separate theological formulations. The New Testament can be understood only if **Jesus**, **Jesus a Christ** and **Jesus the Christ** are differentiated and the distinctions clarified.

Jesus the teacher

Few doubt that Jesus was an historical person. He was a human being who lived and died early in the first century of our era. He was a peasant craftsman who worked and enjoyed social relationships. He was a marvelous storyteller, an itinerant teacher and a preacher of morals and ethics. But he was also an iconoclast. He dared to question the foundational beliefs of the civil and religious systems of his day.

He challenged the traditional religious truths and dogmas of his own ethnic group. He shattered the single most encompassing doctrine of the tradition, the Sabbath. The Sabbath symbolized the covenant and all its ramifications. It was the particular day in which Jews concentrated on their relationship with the supernatural world and recognized their status as a special, chosen people. Their tradition taught that the Sabbath was God's day.

But Jesus said "the Sabbath was made for man and not man for the Sabbath" (Mark 2:27). Jesus avowed that the Sabbath was man's day not God's day. Jesus implied, in fact declared most bluntly, that they should on this day concentrate their attention on human beings and not on the spirits and Gods of the supernatural world. It is a day to think about one's fellow men and the kinds of interaction which make human beings whole.

Jesus shattered the effectiveness of worship, special status and all the rites of purification by which the pious devotees sought to encounter their God. Jesus taught that human beings, not God, were at the center of the holy day.

He did and said things that were equally challenging to the larger civilization. As a member of an ethnic minority group he dared to challenge the hierarchical social structures of the Roman Empire. He called for human equality and declared love rather than obedience to be the central element in the ethical way of life. For Jesus, the foundation of meaningful redemptive social life was love, not subservience. This meant that the principles of hierarchical power structures, whether in this world or the supernatural world, were crippling to the human being. How could the Roman Empire survive without the controls implicit in its hierarchical organization?

There is no doubt he was a troublemaker. He challenged the very foundations of the societies of his day. For this he was executed by the pious leaders of his own religion and the anxious Roman authorities.

During his lifetime Jesus had attracted a following. They were committed to his way of living and interacting, and others joined them. In a few decades this group of "Jesus followers" became something of an influence in the social thinking of the region. They were not Christians. They were followers of Jesus. The doctrines which they taught and the way they lived threatened both religious and civil authorities just as Jesus' life and teachings had threatened authorities a few years earlier.

Jesus a Christ

Saul of Tarsus was one who felt this threat most keenly. He persecuted the followers of Jesus hoping to rid the region of this troublesome social group. But he was troubled by his violent actions toward the followers of Jesus. After a time of intellectual and emotional turmoil he finally changed his mind about them and their purposes. In a marvelous "ah ha" experience he came to see Jesus in a new light.

Saul was well acquainted with the Christs and the messenger myths of antiquity. He knew the Christ principles implicit in some versions of the Messiah in his own ethnic group.

In this moment of light and enlightenment he saw Jesus as a contemporary incarnation of the Christ principle which had been at the core of the messenger myths of antiquity. For Saul a new Christ had come to the world, to his world, even to his own people.

Saul, now named Paul, identified Jesus as a Christ. He then spent the rest of his life promoting this doctrine, founding churches and writing letters which explained his view of Jesus Christ. In his letters Paul applied to this Jesus Christ a wide range of the characteristics and functions of the classical Christs. Terms such as: son of God, king, lord, master, redeemer, savior, advocate, son of man are only a few which are common to Jesus Christ and the Christs of antiquity.

Paul's letters went through many stages of copying, revisions and additions. Errors inevitably occurred and changes were made. In spite of these problems it is evident that Paul saw Jesus as a Christ.

He had never known Jesus as a man. His letters to churches are essentially devoid of any reference to Jesus apart from his death. There is little, if any, awareness of Jesus' stories, parables or wise sayings. His gospel misses Jesus' ministry entirely. He claims only to have known Jesus in some "spiritual way." Some scholars have suggested this to mean a mystical way. [101]

I have contended in the preceding chapters that it was a mythical way. Paul understood Jesus to be a contemporary incarnation, a modern day God-man, with all the characteristics, functions and purposes of previous messenger God-men. Paul's Jesus Christ was an up-to-date version of the mythical Christs with the same message of renewal, rebirth, new life and new hope that had characterized all the Christs of antiquity. Paul promoted his Jesus Christ in this way. He pointed again to the possibilities of human renewal which had been the core message of the myths of antiquity. This is not mystical. There is no mystery. It is mythical! [102]

For Paul the ancient message of the Christs had reappeared. The message was a call to a solid, practical commitment to the potential for real transformation of life. This could be accomplished by grasping the recurring opportunities to change. Most certainly this was consistent with the central message of the myths of antiquity. It was also consistent with many elements in the message and teachings of Jesus.

From this viewpoint Paul's work may provide the opportunity for an enriched understanding of the down-to-earth ethical message of Jesus. Paul saw Jesus as a Christ but he may also have seen that Jesus' teachings had universal significance. There was hope of redemption, rejuvenation, rebirth and new beginnings. For Paul, the central message of the ancient myths was affirmed in Jesus Christ.

In summary, we may say that Paul converted Jesus into a Christ and added him to the roster of mythical Christs. Paul saw Jesus as a contemporary incarnation of the many ancient messengers from the supernatural world. He made Jesus, the man, into a God-man, a supernatural messenger. This was an astounding idea, but not an impossible idea in the Near East of the first century.

Some people believed Paul's doctrine. These people became followers of Paul's "Jesus Christ." As a consequence they were called "Christians" (Acts 11:26). This is a phenomenon significantly different than being a "follower of Jesus."

Paul's discovery of "Jesus Christ" may have been innocent enough. These ideas had validity in the religious culture of the day. But Paul linked Jesus to the Christs in a way which opened the door for profound distortions of the life and work of Jesus, the teacher. Furthermore it opened the door for later theologians to corrupt Paul's mythical "Jesus Christ" in gross and tragic ways. The stage was set in early Christianity for confusions and the compounding of confusions.

Jesus the Christ

The Church fathers struggled with the meaning of Paul's "Jesus Christ." What did this new Christ really mean in the Greco-Roman world? What did "Jesus Christ" mean for the ideological constructs and organizational motifs of Christianity?

In this context a fundamental question had to be asked. "What features of ideology and organization would be most effective in maintaining the allegiance of the converts to Christianity?" What aspects of Paul's "Jesus Christ" would be most relevant to this task? With these purposes in mind ecclesiastical officials, either consciously or unconsciously, began to modify and revise "Jesus a Christ" in a number of significant ways.

First, they began to think of Jesus Christ as a singular and exclusive Christ. Second, they equated myth with fancy and falsehood. Third, they began to think of Jesus Christ not in a mythical way but as a literal and historical God-man.

Jesus Christ an exclusive Christ

The church fathers certainly believed in the supernatural world. They believed that the powers of the supernatural world could intrude in this world. In this they were no different than all their ancestors.

They also knew the theology of the myths of antiquity. In these ancient and universal myths the intruding powers did marvelous things. Human women could be impregnated by the Gods. These women gave birth to God-men. God-men could take human form and therefore be "sons of man." These God-men brought messages of enlightenment to human beings. These Christs struggled with evil powers and were killed. They were resurrected. They ascended to the right hand of the superior Gods, their fathers. They acted as advocates for human beings in the supernatural hall of justice. They mediated the adoption of human beings for eternal association with the Gods in the eternal supernatural world. In that world acceptable human beings became spiritual sons of God and brothers and sisters of the God-men who had been active in their redemption.

These elements of the messenger myths were imbedded in the religious thought of the masses of the people. It was in this kind of intellectual milieu that Paul found the majority of those who accepted his doctrine. These myths were the childhood sacred stories of first generation Christians. For them the transition to Paul's "Jesus Christ" had not been difficult.

But how could the new believers maintain their special version of a new Christ in a social context of traditional mythology? How could they make a meaningful distinction between themselves and the "non believers" who still believed in the old myths but did not believe that Jesus was a Christ?

The problem was even more crucial for the leaders. What could they do to establish and maintain the integrity of a new social group whose ideas and beliefs had so much in common with its neighbors?

The Church leaders concerned with these problems and still unsure about the nature of this new Christ struggled toward ideological and organizational answers. Discussions, debates and conferences occurred. Tremendous differences were found between groups, particularly between those who found Jesus the teacher to be primary and those who found Paul's "Jesus Christ" central to their beliefs.

For those who found the Christ dimensions to be most important, a new interpretation of Jesus Christ emerged.

Paul had taught that Jesus was a Christ in the continuing tradition of the many Christs who had appeared through the ages. Initially the Church fathers agreed with Paul. But Paul had died and as time went on a new conviction emerged, a doctrine which had the power to set them apart from persons who believed in the numerous mythical Christs. They finally concluded that Jesus was not just a Christ, as Paul had implied, but that he was the only Christ.

They rejected all the Christs of the theologies of antiquity. They flew in the face of the myths and scriptures of the general religion of their Greco-Roman culture. In their theologizing they made Paul's Jesus Christ into a unique Christ, a singular and exclusive Christ. He became for them the first Christ, the last Christ, the only Christ. This became a defining difference. This doctrine they promoted and it became the touchstone of orthodoxy.

The exclusive nature of their Jesus Christ was exhibited by a remarkable phrase in the New Testament. Paul had advised Christians to honor Jesus Christ with the words "To the king of ages, immortal, invisible......be honor and glory for ever and ever" (I Timothy 1:17). Such honorific titles and accolades had been addressed to the Christs for thousands of years, particularly in the funnery rituals of the pharaohs. But in the middle of the current version of this Timothy text a remarkable phrase appears: "The only God."

Who among the copiers and revisionists of Paul's writing placed that phrase in the middle of this litany from antiquity? Jesus the Christ was now not only the "only Christ" but also the "only God." What was the purpose of corrupting this ancient litany? Could it be that this doctrine was the capstone that finally separated Christianity from the common tradition?

Jesus Christ was transformed into Jesus the Christ by the Ante-Nicene and Nicene fathers. It was a defining doctrine.

The essence of the matter was encapsulated in the biblical text "There is salvation in no one else, for there is no other name under heaven given among men by which we must be saved" (Acts 4:12).

Having declared a defining difference they sought to reinforce their separation from theologies of antiquity by attacking the concept of "myth."

The Christian perversion of "myth"

Christians had come from a culture where myths provided insight into the nature of relationships with fellow humans and the supernatural world. In their pre-Christian days many church members had a reverence for the myths and had been guided by their moral and spiritual insights. With such a background there was always danger that Christians might be drawn back to traditional religion and the interpretations in which they had been socialized. Such a possibility was a threat to the early church.

The leadership of the church responded to this threat with two arguments. They could not deny the existence of myths but they did argue that myths came from an evil source with evil intent. They argued that the devil had corrupted the minds of the Pagan writers who had produced the myths in order to mislead Christians who would appear later. In a similar way some modern-day Christian Fundamentalists explain fossil remains as the work of the devil that uses them to plant doubt in the minds of the faithful about the processes of creation.

In addition the church fathers began to interpret "myth" in a way entirely foreign to the meaning of myth as it was understood in the ancient world and as it is used in literary analysis today. They began to look at "myths" as fanciful fiction, interesting and amusing but without meaning and therefore irrelevant; maybe even misleading and therefore dangerous.

The early church fathers had made Jesus Christ into an only Christ and had rejected myths as false, valueless and the work of the devil. What were they to do with the mythical dimensions of Paul's Jesus Christ?

"Jesus <u>the</u> Christ" becomes a literal Christ

The leaders of the early church had made Jesus Christ into an exclusive Christ. But his characteristics, functions and powers were identical to the Christs of antiquity. In their efforts to distance their religion from its genetic source they developed a remarkable doctrine. They declared Jesus Christ to be real. They declared all the attributes, characteristics and functions also to be real, literal and historical.

The critical elements in the mythological Christs of antiquity have been extensively described in previous chapters. Six of the most crucial might be: birth, death, blood sacrifice, resurrection, ascension and salvation.

In the myths these were symbolic. But the church fathers demonized myths. So their singular and exclusive Jesus Christ and all his Christly features and functions had to be real and literal. They made everything about Jesus Christ into history.

In the final analysis, for them, all the following statements were concrete, literal and real. There was a real divine impregnation of the human woman Mary. A God-man was born who was, at the same time and in the same body, both God and man. This God-man was killed by real enemies. but with the collusion of his supernatural father. Real literal blood flowed from his body. This real and literal blood had properties which, in some way saves human beings from sin and its consequences. Jesus the Christ really and literally rose from the dead. He really and literally ascended into the supernatural world. He really and literally will return to this earth some day. He will pass final judgment on all human beings. He will be at the right hand of his father and welcome the faithful to a real heaven for all eternity.

CHAPTER 9

SALVATION AND THE NATURE OF TRUTH

The church fathers of the second, third and fourth centuries were developing their conceptions of the characteristics, functions and purposes of "Jesus the Christ." But even these conceptions and interpretations were not uniform. There was much controversy and frequent schisms.

Other problems arose because some of the church fathers understood Jesus Christ in various mythological ways but distinct from the mythological Christs of antiquity. Thus there were many alternative ways of thinking about both Jesus and Jesus Christ. Some saw Jesus Christ as consistent with the Christs of antiquity in the mode of Paul's theology. Others declared themselves to be followers of Jesus and paid little attention to the Christs or the doctrines of the church fathers.

Can truth be divided? Can truth encompass contradictions and even opposites? Does truth consist of absolutes and if it does, whose "truth" is true?

Relationships in the early church were fraught with contention and division. In more than three centuries no consensus was ever reached about the meaning of it all.

The Official Formulation of Truth

Christianity had become widespread in the Roman Empire by the fourth century. Although it was fragmented it was a growing social movement. Variant interpretations of "Jesus,"

"Jesus a Christ" and "Jesus the Christ" produced turmoil, division and hostile subgroups.

All this was disruptive to peace and civic order. Emperor Constantine, fearing for the stability of his Empire, ordered a conclave of church leaders to resolve the theological differences. Constantine hoped thereby to bring harmony to the church, fend off the threatening schisms and restore social order. To facilitate this conference he provided free and safe conveyance for the bishops who were willing to attend. Roman legions provided security at the conference. The meetings took place in the city of Nicaea on the eastern shores of the Adriatic Sea in 325 CE. Emperor Constantine himself, although a pagan, made the keynote address at this church conference.

The Nicene Creed

After long and contentious debate the bishops who attended the conference adopted summary statements of belief. These were doctrines the bishops had been developing through decades of time. They finally declared a series of dogmas to be true, orthodox and obligatory for anyone who claimed to be Christian. Some of the crucial doctrines were incorporated in a document which emerged from the conference. This document is known as the Nicene Creed.

"We believe in one God, the Father, the Almighty, maker of heaven and earth, of all that is, both seen and unseen. We believe in one Lord, Jesus Christ, the only Son of God eternally begotten of the Father, God from God, Light from Light, true God from true God, begotten, not made, one in Being with the Father. Through him all things were made. For us men and for our salvation he came down from heaven. By the power of the Holy Spirit he was born of the Virgin Mary, and became man. For our sake he was crucified under Pontius Pilate; he suffered, died, and was buried. On the third day he rose again in fulfillment of the

Scriptures. He ascended into heaven and is seated at the right hand of the Father. He will come again in glory to judge the living and the dead, and his kingdom will have no end. We believe in the Holy Spirit, the Lord, the giver of life, who proceeds from the Father and the Son. With the Father and Son he is worshiped and glorified. He has spoken through the prophets. We believe in one holy catholic and apostolic Church. We acknowledge one baptism for the forgiveness of sins. We look for the resurrection of the dead, and the life of the world to come. Amen."

The Apostle's Creed

An earlier Creed, the Apostles Creed, was used widely in the early church as an indoctrination tool. Catechumens were required to affirm their belief in the doctrines of this creed.

"I believe in God, the Father almighty, creator of heaven and earth. I believe in Jesus Christ, his only Son, our Lord. He was conceived by the power of the Holy Spirit and born of the Virgin Mary. He suffered under Pontius Pilate, was crucified, died, and was buried. He descended into hell. On the third day he rose again. He ascended into heaven and is seated at the right hand of the Father. He will come again to judge the living and the dead. I believe in the Holy Spirit, the holy catholic Church, the communion of saints, the forgiveness of sins, the resurrection of the body, and the life everlasting."

The persistence of Creeds

Many of these doctrines, as indicated in previous chapters, had antecedents in the Near Eastern theologies in the centuries before Jesus. They have many similarities to Egyptian and Persian theological doctrines from even earlier times.

The Apostolic Creed and the Nicene Creed are still the most widely used Creeds in Catholic and Protestant churches to this day. A number of other creeds were developed in following centuries which attempted to clarify and expand some of the doctrines which appear in these Creeds.

Selection of the Canon

The bishops, who had attended the conference at Nicaea, had come to an agreement about the "truth" and presented it in the creedal doctrines. But a basic problem remained as a hindrance to unity. The doctrines themselves were based on theological formulations contained in documents circulating through the churches.

By the fourth century various kinds of manuscripts "gospels," "saying," "letters," "essays," "theological treatises" and other materials relative to "Jesus," "Jesus a Christ" and "Jesus the Christ" were being read and studied. These scriptures were marvelously diverse, often contradictory and reflective of vast theological difference. As long as these theologically diverse materials were being interpreted, studied and reinterpreted how was unity ever to be attained? The bishops responded to this problem.

They set themselves the task of selecting from this plethora of scriptures those materials which they considered to be authoritative for teaching, preaching and reaching theological unity. The 27 documents which they selected are the books of the New Testament. This body of material is generally referred to as "the canon." All other scriptures were declared to be undependable or even heretical.

By the time the materials were selected and the canon closed, Jesus Christ was presented as an exclusive Christ. He was portrayed as absolutely unique and singular. He was reported to be "the only begotten son" (John 1:18) and even "the only God" (I Timothy 1:17).

Moreover Jesus Christ was no longer a myth. All the mythical elements had been literalized. All the functions of the Christs of antiquity had been made concrete and literal.

Is it surprising that the documents selected by the bishops reflect the doctrines of the creeds which they formulated? Is it surprising that these documents have language and theology consistent with the doctrinal formulations of the particular coterie of bishops who were participants at the conference? It was these bishops who selected materials from dozens of possibilities and declared their selection to be uniquely authoritative. Church leaders finally declared these books to be the "Word of God."

In the minds of the church fathers this canon laid the foundation for unity. Could they have anticipated the controversy, confusion and disunity which their "unifying" documents would produce into the 21st century?

Creedal Salvation

Most of the doctrines set forth in the creeds are inexplicable to the human mind. They are beyond human understanding. Apart from death there is nothing to which we can relate. We have no data remotely supportive of any of these dogmas. They were inexplicable even to the church fathers as witnessed by the thousands of pages in which they were endlessly discussed with the most amazing and confusing explanations.[103]

In the final analysis the fathers concluded that "believing" is crucial; not "understanding." To be saved and go to heaven one must believe that these theological formulations ensconced in the creeds are literally and historically true. Believing these doctrines is critical to becoming a child of God. One must give mental assent to the proposition that the events reported by these statements actually happened and have eternal and supernatural consequences.

The Incomprehensible plan of the Incomprehensible God

According to the creeds God designed this program of inexplicable events as a means to take away the sin of the world, purify human spirits and souls, save them from hell and make them fit to associate with the eternal spirits in the supernatural world. This is the "plan of salvation."

This plan is beyond human comprehension. It defies any logic. No human being can understand this complex of events. Neither can any human understand how these events produce salvation. But it is this incomprehensibility which is the genius of the plan!

It is God's plan. He designed it. He alone understands it. He alone knows how it works.[104] This is the crux of the matter and ties all the inscrutable doctrines together. God designed his plan of salvation in such a way that the human has one obligation. This "plan of salvation" takes effect for human beings when they give mental agreement to the truth of the creedal propositions.

This "believing" process, in the context of Christian theology, is sometimes called "faith."[105] If a human being has faith of this kind the plan of salvation takes effect. If a human does not believe in these crucial doctrines the plan of salvation does not work. The human being is then left to the consequences of sin in this world and the next.

What is amazing in all this is that the bishops consistently resisted the reality of the source of their doctrines. However, we probably should not be surprised. The churches of our day fail to see, or refuse to admit, the commonalities with the theologies of antiquity.

At any rate, for some segments of Christianity, the transformation of Jesus Christ from myth to history was complete. It was no longer possible to ask the question; "What do the myths and stories of antiquity really mean?"

The Counsel of Nicaea, convened by Emperor Constantine laid the foundation for an enveloping, unthinking belief system with dire ramifications for the western world!

Jesus disappeared from the Constantinian church

By the fourth century Jesus, man, teacher, preacher and storyteller was rarely the focus of theological work. His ethical message no longer really mattered. His life and work for redemptive interpersonal and social relationships were essentially forgotten.

What did matter, for the church, was an exclusive Christ engaged in a literal way at all the crucial points in the "plan of salvation." The Christ myth had been converted to history. Jesus and his message had essentially disappeared.

CHAPTER 10

A SUMMARY:
JESUS OR CHRIST IN THE EARLY CHURCH

Paul had identified Jesus with the Christs of antiquity. The implications of this discovery inspired endless debates and thousands of pages of commentary for centuries.

The Social Context of Early Christian Literature

In the later part of the first century and early in the second century numerous essays, letters and documents were circulating purporting to describe the life and teaching of Jesus of Nazareth. Some scholars have concluded that the "sayings of Jesus" were among the earliest of written materials about Jesus. Some scholars suggest that scriptures such as Q and other materials common to Mark, Luke and Mathew were written by the middle of the first century.

None of these original writings have been found. The documents, essays and letters which we have in the New Testament are copies. They did not come into their current form until the second or third centuries at the earliest. Decades, generations, even centuries had passed since the life, teaching and crucifixion of Jesus.

The passage of time, even a few years, has a tendency to modify the perception of events. If we are to understand the New Testament materials we must be aware they are products of faulty memory and copying errors. But more importantly they are the products of interpretation, emphases, reformulation and shaping by the social and theological perceptions of those who made copies. Luke alludes to this problem in the introduction to his essay.[106]

The letters of Paul were among the early writings of the New Testament. They are largely theological ruminations and treatises on ethics and morals. The fourth gospel, in its first version, was probably written in the second century and is even more explicitly and deliberately a theological analysis.

These and other materials in the canon were constructed in a world of great diversity, confusion and contending philosophical and religious ideas. Some wrote about Jesus of Nazareth, the marvelous storyteller and friend of the poor. Others perceived him to have special miraculous powers. Some of his earliest disciples thought of him as a special man, even something of a heroic man. Saul of Tarsus wrote from the perspective of one who believed in messengers from the supernatural world; the God-men, the Christs of the myths of antiquity. All these perspectives are understandable in the social world of the first and second centuries.

With such diverse understandings of Jesus, the stage was set for disagreements and controversy in the church of the second, third and fourth centuries. In these three hundred years different kinds of scriptures appeared, written from many different perspectives. These were followed by analyses, interpretations, sharpening and elaborations. Some writers, following Paul's lead, attempted to explain Jesus in the context of the Christ models of antiquity.

Priests and bishops, some of whom were theologians, grappled with these materials and wrote their own interpretations. Some of these may be found in what we know today as the writings of the Apostolic, Ante-Nicene, Nicene and Post-Nicene Fathers. However, alternate interpretations were produced in these centuries. Some were lost. Some were deliberately destroyed. The theological viewpoints of these destroyed materials can be inferred from the efforts of the church fathers to refute the interpretations with which they disagreed. Some of the "lost" documents have come to light in modern times.

Religious literature like any other literature is inevitably shaped by the social conditions and cultural orientations of the writers. Thus the writings about Jesus and Christianity are remarkably diverse.[107] In addition the ideologies which guide people and the purposes which motivate them are dynamic forces in the shaping of interpretations and viewpoints.

What religious literature says about life is marvelously interesting. But the reason people believe and say what they do is even more interesting. Why did the church fathers write the things they wrote? Why did they make the interpretations evident in their writings? Why did they keep some writings and destroy others? The answers to these questions are crucial to understanding the New Testament and Christianity.

But these questions are rarely asked. The answers threaten tradition and the securities which tradition provides. However the answers to these kinds of questions may lead to an understanding of the social processes which produced medieval Christianity, the dark ages and the debilitating confusions and animosities in contemporary Christianity.

The Confusion of Three Entities

I have suggested that in the New Testament, non-canonical scriptures, vast sets of commentaries and even 21st century religious debates there are three fundamentally different perceptions of Jesus. We might hypothesize that these are three distinct social constructs, three exclusive religious entities, three unique theological propositions. Furthermore, they are all misunderstood and mixed together in most confusing ways.

First we have "**Jesus**," the man of Nazareth, the itinerant philosopher, storyteller and teacher of a universal ethic of love.

Second, we have "**Jesus <u>a</u> Christ**," a supernatural messenger and savior who exhibits all the essential characteristics of the numerous God-men or Christs of antiquity. It is this Jesus Christ who was promoted by Paul.

Third, we have "**Jesus <u>the</u> Christ**," the singular exclusive, literal, historical Christ produced by the theologizing of the Ante-Nicene and Nicene fathers and canonized by church counsels in the fourth and fifth centuries.

These entities, these religious concepts, these mental constructs are worlds apart! They are distinctly different realities. Yet among Christians there is a desperate effort to link them. This has been and continues to be the agony of preachers, Bible teachers, theologians, seminary professors and some scholars of religion in academia.[108]

Jesus the teacher had lived and been executed. Paul had linked Jesus with the Christs of antiquity and named this particular Christ "Jesus Christ." The church fathers, in their theologizing transformed Paul's Jesus Christ into an exclusive and only Christ, "Jesus <u>the</u> Christ." This Christ has many similarities to the "Jesus Christ" of modern day Christianity. [109]

How did this all come about? The answers must be found in the social settings and social struggles of powerful people in the early church.

Jesus the teacher of redemptive love

Jesus the itinerant teacher and preacher of Galilee taught and practiced a lifestyle of love and forgiveness. His redemptive interaction with his fellowmen brought healing and hope to those who followed his way. He challenged the dehumanizing religious and political dogmatisms of his day. For this he was executed.

The "followers of Jesus" were attracted by the remarkable universal ethic which Jesus taught and demonstrated. This ethical concern persisted among followers of Jesus in succeeding generations. One may still find it even among some who insist on calling themselves "Christian."[110]

But for the vast majority who call themselves "Christian" there is a different story.

Jesus a Christ and the Emergence of Christianity

Their story does not begin with Jesus! It begins a generation after the crucifixion of Jesus. It begins in the seventh decade of the first century as they were converted to the teachings of Paul of Tarsus. Under the impact of the "Jesus Christ" doctrine preached by Paul, a few Jesus followers and a group of gentiles were transformed into a cult called "Christians."[111] They were a religious social group in a Greco-Roman world.

Two significant dimensions of this culture had influenced all of them. The religious and philosophical thought of this culture understood the world and the supernatural world in mythological terms. At the core of this understanding was the conviction and certainty that the supernatural world intruded into this world. God-men, anointed ones, messengers or Christs were important manifestations of this intrusion.

The second feature of this culture was the efficient hierarchical structure of all social institutions. This was the administrative model familiar to everyone and it was adopted by the developing Christian Church.

All religious groups in the first century recognized the existence of many Gods and many Christs but tended to be devoted to particular deities, There were temples, worship sites and rituals honoring Diana, Dionysius, Cebele, Isis, Osiris, Mithras and many others. In the seventh decade "Jesus Christ" was added to this list. Each deity had their own particular group of devotees and rituals. Those who worshiped "Jesus Christ" were called Christians.

This early church was small and relatively powerless. It was under threat from many directions. Survival depended on an enlarged membership. Paul's missionary activity was directed at this problem.

The development of special characteristics is critical to the survival of a social group. The establishment of social boundaries creates a sense of group identity and integrity.

Unique doctrines and the profanation of alternative ideas were powerful devices in the formation of the early church. A claim to exclusive supernatural truth and the rejection of alternative doctrines created unbridgeable gaps. The "in-group" was "God's people." The "out-group" was "not God's people." The later were defined as unbelievers, dangerous and damned; conditions to which terms like "heretic" or "pagan" could be applied.

The Exclusive and Literal Christ, Jesus the Christ

Christians rejected the Gods and the Christs of their neighbors. They concentrated not on Jesus but on Jesus Christ. They identified Jesus Christ as an only begotten son of God and even as the only Christ. Thus the Ante-Nicene fathers created a singular and exclusive Christ, "Jesus the Christ." As they constructed this new Christ it was helpful to deny even the mythological reality of any other Christs. This became the fulcrum on which religious destiny turned. In this they went far beyond Paul.

The Nicene fathers transformed Jesus Christ into a singular and exclusive Christ. They also transformed him into a literal and historical Christ. All the common characteristics and functions of the mythological Christs of antiquity were made literal and historical in this only Christ of all time.

He became a son of God and a son of man by virtue of a God induced impregnation of a human woman. This God-man was crucified by human enemies but, as the key event in the plan of salvation, this execution was also planned and willed by his supernatural father. Blood flowed from his body. In some way this literal blood produces purification, new life and salvation. There is a literal resurrection and a literal transport to a literal heaven to live a literal spiritual life at the right hand of the father. In this position of power Jesus the Christ will welcome the humans who believe these doctrines.

For the bishops all this was real. It was and is Gods' plan of salvation. The human responsibility in this complex "salvation plan" was to intellectually accept the historical, literal reality of it all. Sometimes this "believing" activity is called "faith."

The ante-Nicene and Nicene fathers understood Jesus Christ in an exclusive, literal and historical way. As the western church – organized on the Roman hierarchical model of administration – gained wealth, its primary bishops gained power. They came to see their own interpretations as truth and their power enabled them to suppress alternative interpretations.

Struggle against Heretics

There were multitudes of alternate understandings. Many individuals and communities paid little attention to the doctrines described above but believed and lived the universal ethic which Jesus, the man, had taught and practiced. There were other communities who believed Jesus

Christ should be understood in a mythological way. Many from these different persuasions wrote treatises setting forth their viewpoints and interpretations.

The debates encompassed every nuance of interpretation imaginable. This religious confusion had significant ramifications for the stability of the Roman Empire.

To deal with this condition and to attempt to produce some unity in the emerging Christian movement the powerful bishops took action. They declared certain interpretations to be true and all others false. Thousands of pages written by the church fathers describe in detail the nature of heretical ideas, often quoting from the writings of their opponents. The pages are full of refutations and laden with denunciations of those who differed.

Those who dared to entertain interpretations contrary to the definitions of the powerful church fathers were declared to be heretics. They were harassed, persecuted, deprived of office, sometimes banished or killed. Their writings became the object of ridicule and destruction. The dehumanizing consequences of this church activity were bloody and almost endless.

Please search in the mass of material produced by the Apostolic, Ante-Nicene, Nicene and Post-Nicene Fathers for their diatribes against heretics.[112]

A few examples will introduce us to this tragic dimension of church history.

By the second century the Apostolic fathers and early Ante-Nicene fathers were engaged in massive efforts to suppress viewpoints different than their own.[113] Irenaeus, a student of Polycarp became bishop in Lyon in Gaul during the second century. He, like his teacher, wrote extensively against the doctrines of the Docetists declaring them to be "heretics."[114] Polycarp labeled them "antichrist."[115]

Tertullian, Bishop of Carthage early in the third century wrote extensively in opposition to those who promoted doctrines at variance with his own. In a document entitled _Prescriptions against Heretics_ he observes: "heretics not being Christians, but rather perverters of Christ's teachings, may not claim the Christian scriptures, committed to and carefully kept by the Church."[116]

As a leading bishop Tertullian affirmed the authority of the church to determine what doctrines were orthodox and what beliefs were perverse. He does not specify what the Christian scriptures were but refused to let those who disagreed with him use them to explain their variant interpretations. This kind of mind control was well developed and extensively used by the early church fathers.

St Augustine in his fourth century book "_The City of God_" quotes the Roman Pagan Varro: "There are many things that are true which is not useful for the vulgar crowd to know; and certain things, although they are false, it is expedient for the people to believe."[117]

Augustine is quoting Varro in order to ridicule this doctrine. But with slight variation it is the very principle which guided Augustine in the selection of dogmas which church members must know and believe. [118]

Augustine had his own formula for instruction and education in the church. He decided what was true and what was false. He utterly failed to recognize that the contents of these categories were simply the products of his own speculations; speculations which were heavily dependent on the theologies of antiquity. The formulas of Varro and Augustine had no consequential difference. Varro recognized what he was doing. Augustine and the Church fathers did not recognize what they were doing to the people.

The Church fathers encapsulated their "truth" in doctrines and required church members to believe these dogmas. They also defined what was false. Falsehood was any doctrine at variance with their conception of truth. Anyone holding alternate doctrines was not a Christian.

These were the guiding principles of the Church fathers as they formed and preserved "Constantinian Christianity."[119] It was the way to preserve what they believed to be true. It was the way to control the "Christian" adherents. It was the way in which church administrators maintained their power.

The formula of Augustine was certainly the mindset of the church fathers in 325 CE as they met in conference at Nicaea for the purpose of selecting the authoritative scriptures; the books which appear in the New Testament. It was the guiding principle in the formation of the creeds which defined the nature of Jesus Christ for the next millennium and longer. The church fathers controlled the "truth" and made it available. They determined what was "false" and suppressed it.

In spite of their efforts to control "truth" and exclude "falsehood" they were not entirely successful. There were social leaders, both in the church and outside the church, who had other convictions and whose definition of truth and falsehood was different.

Attempts to Create Unity in Early Christianity

The Edict of Toleration made Christianity legal in 313 CE and the numbers of Christians grew. However this did nothing to reduce conflict in the church or bring peace to the Empire. The counsel of Nicaea had made two major efforts to unify the church: the creedal formulation of numerous doctrines and the selection of authoritative documents. These measures had some success in those portions of the empire most closely controlled by the Roman bishops. In these regions the church members were culturally Roman and responsive to hierarchical organizational structures imposed by church administrators.

In spite of the efforts of Emperor Constantine and the bishops at the counsel of Nicaea to unify the church and impose Christianity on the population, alternate interpretations of Jesus and Jesus Christ flourished in many regions. These alternate understandings caused disagreements and continuing conflicts. Church officials, in succeeding decades sought to impose unity by additional doctrinal statements and creeds.

Finally, under the reign of Theodosius the Great (379-395) Christianity became the official religion of the Roman Empire. The relationship between the state and the Christian church was cemented. The religious, political and military institutions of the empire were employed by the church to impose Christianity.[120]

One example of the religious efforts to impose Christianity is represented by the Athenasian Creed written about 500 CE. One version has 44 items. The controlling features are explicit in the first two and the last items.

The Athenasian Creed: [Alternate readings in brackets][121]

1. *Whosoever will be saved, before all things it is necessary that he hold the Catholic Faith.*

2. *Which Faith except everyone do keep whole and undefiled, without doubt he shall perish everlastingly.*

3. *And the Catholic Faith is this: that we worship one God in Trinity, and Trinity in Unity,*

4. *Neither confounding the Persons, nor dividing the Substance [Essence].*

5. *For there is one Person of the Father, another of the Son, and another of the Holy Ghost.*

6. *But the Godhead of the Father, of the Son, and of the Holy Ghost, is all one, the Glory equal, the Majesty co-eternal.*

7. *Such as the Father is, such is the Son, and such is the Holy Ghost.*

8. *The Father uncreate [uncreated], the Son uncreate [uncreated], and the Holy Ghost uncreate [uncreated].*

9. *The Father incomprehensible [unlimited], the Son incomprehensible [unlimited], and the Holy Ghost incomprehensible [unlimited].*

10. *The Father eternal, the Son eternal, and the Holy Ghost eternal.*

11. *And yet they are not three eternals, but one eternal.*

12. *As also there are not three incomprehensibles [infinites], nor three uncreated, but one uncreated, and one incomprehensible [infinite].*

13. *So likewise the Father is Almighty, the Son Almighty, and the Holy Ghost Almighty.*

14. *And yet they are not three Almighties, but one Almighty.*

15. *So the Father is God, the Son is God, and the Holy Ghost is God.*

16. *And yet they are not three Gods, but one God.*

17. *So likewise the Father is Lord, the Son Lord, and the Holy Ghost Lord.*

18. *And yet not three Lords, but one Lord.*

19. *For like as we are compelled by the Christian verity: to acknowledge every Person by himself to be both God and Lord.*

20. *So are we forbidden by the Catholic Religion, to say, There be [are] three Gods, or three Lords.*

21. *The Father is made of none, neither created, nor begotten.*

22. *The Son is of the Father alone, not made, nor created, but begotten.*

23. *The Holy Ghost is of the Father and of the Son, neither made, nor created, nor begotten, but proceeding.*

24. *So there is one Father, not three Fathers; one Son, not three Sons; one Holy Ghost, not three Holy Ghosts.*

25. *And in this Trinity none is afore, or after other; none is greater, or less than another [there is nothing before, or after: nothing greater or less];*

26. *But the whole three Persons are co-eternal together and co-equal.*

27. *So that in all things, as is aforesaid, the Unity in Trinity and the Trinity in Unity is to be worshipped.*

28. *He therefore that will be saved must [let him] thus think of the Trinity.*

29. *Furthermore, it is necessary to everlasting salvation that he also believe rightly the Incarnation of our Lord Jesus Christ.*

30. *For the right Faith is, that we believe and confess, that our Lord Jesus Christ, the Son of God, is God and Man.*

31. *God, of the Substance [Essence] of the Father, begotten before the worlds; and Man, of the Substance [Essence] of his Mother, born in the world;*

32. *Perfect God and perfect Man, of a reasonable soul and human flesh subsisting.*

33. *Equal to the Father, as touching his Godhead; and inferior to the Father, as touching his Manhood.*

34. *Who although he be [is] God and Man, yet he is not two, but one Christ.*

35. *One, not by conversion of the Godhead into flesh, but by taking assumption of the Manhood into God.*

36. *One altogether, not by confusion of Substance [Essence], but by unity of Person.*

37. *For as the reasonable soul and flesh is one man, so God and Man is one Christ;*

38. *Who suffered for our salvation, descended into hell [Hades, spirit-world], rose again the third day from the dead.*

39. *He ascended into heaven, he sitteth on the right hand of the Father, God [God the Father] Almighty,*

40. *From whence [thence] he shall come to judge the quick and the dead.*

41. *At whose coming all men shall rise again with their bodies*

42. *And shall give account for their own works.*

43. *And they that have done good shall go into life everlasting, and they that have done evil into everlasting fire.*

44. *This is the Catholic Faith, which except a man believe faithfully [truly and firmly], he cannot be saved.*

What is the intent of this Creed? What might the social consequences be? Would it frighten people into a specific kind of Christianity? Does it clarify the concept of the Trinity? Does the "Plan of Salvation" make sense to any human being?

Those acquainted with Neo-Platonic thought will recognize the efforts to probe below form in the search for substance. They will recognize gradations of emanations from the ultimately unknowable substance. They might even appreciate the mental constructs of this creed which attempt to bring perfect unity out of total complexity.

The meaning of the statements in this creed might have been consistent with Neo-Platonic thought. It is doubtful if the masses of Christians understood them. Did the authors, themselves, really understand the propositions which they had written? Do Christians today understand these doctrines?

Athenasius with other Church fathers apparently felt it necessary to make the confusing complex of ideas a matter of belief rather than understanding. And they made this belief the instrument of salvation. In item 44 the insertion (*truly and firmly*) even specified the quality of belief required.

The adherents of this kind of Christianity were doomed to intellectual confusion! They were also doomed to hell unless they "truly and firmly" believed these propositions. Those who could not believe were heretics.

But this is not the whole story of the social world of the early church.

Struggle against Pagans

Christianity, although it was troublesome to the Roman Empire was still a minor religious movement in its first centuries. The Greco-Roman world was pagan, even Constantine, in spite of his political and military use of Christianity, remained a pagan until his dying days.

The myths of antiquity had remarkable power in the life of the masses. There was always the possibility that those who had become Christians would be enticed back to the old ways of thinking and believing.[122]

From the very beginning pagan perceptions of the world were a threat to the emerging power of the Church fathers. For four hundred years their struggle against paganism went on in concert with the struggle against heresy within the church. This is a marvelously bloody story full of intrigue and prevarication. There were two foci.

For the bishops of the church all truth about the supernatural world and its relationship to this world was revealed in Jesus the Christ as they understood this concept. Therefore any interpretations of ancient myths and any understandings of the supernatural world prior to the appearance of their singular Christ were false. This exclusive Christ event was for them a true watershed. Pagan and false became synonymous. Thus the mythologies which had sustained social groups and civilizations for centuries were anathema.

The second focus of the church engaged the intellectuals of the pagan world. The vast body of knowledge accumulated through centuries was preserved and nourished in the libraries, museums, academies, schools and other centers of learning scattered about the known world. These repositories of wisdom and knowledge; these institutions of research and study posed a constant threat to the "absolute truths" promoted by the powerful administrators of what became the Constantinian Church. The vast learning of antiquity and its intellectuals became objects of envy, fear and hatred.

At the core of this anxiety and hostility was all the data presented by pagan philosophers. These intellectuals had proven conclusively that the characteristics and functions which the church attributed exclusively to their Christ had been present in the various myths and Christs of antiquity? The pagan philosophers badgered the bishops with the observation that there was nothing new in Christianity except its exclusiveness.

The church waged war against pagan centers of learning. As the power of the church increased, the assault on the centers of learning increased. Two examples at the turn of the fifth century provide a glimpse of Christian techniques for the suppression and destruction of knowledge and learning.

The library at Alexandria, Egypt, was inspired by Alexander the Great and constructed by his friend Ptolemy in the fourth century BCE. It contained, by various estimates between 500,000 and 750,000 manuscripts on every conceivable field of knowledge in the ancient world.[123]

This library was not only a repository of manuscripts; it was also a center of learning which drew scholars from the Near East and the Western world. It was the place where Jewish Scholars translated their scriptures to the Septuagint version. It was a teaching and research institution with tremendous resources and the most brilliant minds in the early centuries of our era.[124]

In 400 CE the Serapeum, a branch library to which many of the books had been moved for security reasons was burned on the order of Theophilus, the Bishop of Alexandria. Fifteen years later a Christian mob with the connivance of Bishop Cyril, the successor to Theophilus, burned all that remained of the library collection, and destroyed the buildings of that marvelous institution of higher learning. In addition this bishop was implicated in the murder of the brilliant mathematician, Hypathia, the leading female philosopher at that remarkable institution.[125]

The Academy of Plato in Athens, founded in 387 BCE persisted into the sixth century CE. It was for 900 years a repository of ancient wisdom and a center of research and learning particularly in the philosophy of mathematics. It was closed in the name of Christianity by Emperor Justinian in 529 CE, its faculty forced to flee and those who failed to escape were killed.[126]

These two cases illustrate the relentless and extensive efforts of the church to destroy the accumulated knowledge and wisdom of centuries. Truth and knowledge for the church by the end of the fifth century CE was circumscribed by its own doctrines and creeds. Nothing else was true and the dark ages ensued.

Some of this spirit and behavior is latent in some forms of Christianity. We may be witnessing its revival in the 21st century.

Questions for Contemporary Christian Theologians

Where is Jesus in all of this? Does the "Jesus Christ" of the fifth century, in whose name learning was destroyed and truth confined to creeds, have any connection to Jesus, the promoter of a universal ethic. Does the "Jesus Christ" of the Creeds have any relevance to the "Jesus Christ" of Paul or the New Testament? Does the "Jesus Christ" of Paul have any relevance to Jesus, the man of Galilee, who taught us how to love and live? Where is Jesus in 21st century Christianity?

Chapter 11

A Range of Responses

The discussion of the social and cultural creation of Christianity in the preceding chapters will elicit a range of responses.

Over the years I have personally had a wide range of responses to the theological ideas presented in this book. At different times in my faith journey, I would have fit into some of the response categories defined below.

I have experienced securities and endured uncertainties as I contemplated the implications of traditional Christian doctrines. I have experienced the fear of alternatives and the emotional pain of transition.

Through my youth, college and seminary years, time as a pastor, years in a counseling agency and many years of teaching in a college setting, I've become aware of the spiritual agonies of people who struggle with matters of belief and faith. Many have experienced a spiritual journey similar to mine. They have testified to their pain in the context of various forms of belief systems and expressed the relief they felt as they encountered new insights and developed the courage to change.

Spiritual growth is a gradual process and we all find ourselves at different places on the continuum. Perhaps you will see yourself in one or more of these responses.

A. I reject the ideas in this book absolutely and completely.

I reject the theses of this book. I do this because truth lies in the doctrines of traditional Creedal Christianity. The hypotheses suggested here regarding the supernatural world and the Bible are dangerous, evil, come from the devil and will inevitably result in the judgment of God and eternal damnation.

I am aware that the doctrines of the church are incomprehensible to human beings. What God does is beyond the reach of human intellectual thought. "God so loved the world that he gave his only begotten son, that whoever believes in him should not perish but have everlasting life" (John 3:16). God's plan of salvation is clear. It is illogical and incomprehensible; in fact it is foolishness to the human mind. But I am saved by faith, not by sight or understanding.

This marvelous plan of salvation is proof enough of the power and love of God.

The book, _Jesus or Christ?_, sows doubt in the minds of believers.

The Bible is the "word of God." God would not lie to us. I rest secure in this knowledge. It is my God-given task to refute the arguments of "unbelievers," try to convert them and lead them to salvation.

B. I respond to these ideas with increased fear and anxiety.

I am already hounded by an undercurrent of doubt. The theses of the book, _Jesus or Christ?_, add to my confusion. The Bible, creeds, confessions of faith, liturgical materials and hymn texts are confusing, contradictory and

126

incomprehensible. Any attempt to apply logic or scientific methodology inevitably leads to more doubt.

I realize that there are different interpretations of the Bible and different understandings of Jesus Christ. My church, my friends and my larger social group generally have traditional Christian beliefs. We know that "false teachers" are common. These false teachers write books and preach sermons.

I cling to traditional doctrines. But sometimes I am confused, mystified and anxious.

To counteract this confusion, I seek affirmation of my traditional beliefs from every possible source. I know that God knows everything. He designed the plan of salvation. I am saved because I believe in the plan of salvation.

But even as I struggle to believe more firmly, doubts keep cropping up. At such times a profound question disturbs my mind and soul. "What is wrong with me that I lack the certainty of faith to which some other people testify?"

I try to rectify this lack of faith with confession, prayer, meditation, Bible reading and a whole range of pious attitudes and activities. I go to revival meetings and have been "saved" several times. I know that God will not withhold his mercy from the truly faithful. I keep searching for the sins which hinder me from a mature faith. Have I committed the unpardonable sin?

What if the theses of this book are true? Where would I be then? Is there no God or Heaven or Hell? What would keep me moral?

My God, is there nothing more than this spiritual pain. Would it help if I would testify more boldly to God's mercy and salvation plan? Would it help if I could convert some "unbelievers?"

C. Intellectually I appreciate many of the ideas in this book, but I reject the application to Christianity.

I have a dual reaction to this book. I have been exposed to many theological perspectives. I recognize the relevance of mythological materials in an understanding of ancient and non-Christian cultures. But I reject the application of these critical intellectual processes to Christianity.

Christianity is a unique religion. It seems to respond to basic human dilemmas in a more comprehensive way than other religions. It seems to me that the Bible testifies to a markedly more beneficent God than the gods of the pagans.

Other religions claim to have messengers from the supernatural world. But their Christs are remarkably different than Jesus Christ.

I know that the Bible is religious literature and was produced in a variety of cultural settings. However I believe it is unique in some special way. I have looked at the complexities and contradictions and am aware of a wide range of interpretations. This makes the Bible a remarkable book. It engages the human mind in a wealth of possibilities.

Through many years of studying the Bible, I have analyzed the words and phrases in the original languages and have been thrilled and exhilarated with the insights and multiple nuances available there. In my studies, I have found much data supporting traditional beliefs. This evidence is sufficient to temper any doubts and anxieties which *Jesus or Christ?* raises.

Moreover a traditional understanding of the Bible has undergirded the thinking of millions and provided the worldview of enduring societies through many centuries. I cannot fly in the face of such evidence.

I recognize the logic of non-traditional interpretations of the Bible and am willing to discuss these interesting ideas with fellow theologians and academics. However, as leaders we must remember our responsibility to the church community. Most of my fellow Christians hold traditional beliefs. Why raise questions about faith and belief? There are too many uncertainties in life as it is. The loving and Christian thing to do is to avoid discussions which raise doubts and produce anxieties.

Some of the ideas in this book, *Jesus or Christ?*, raise intriguing questions and open new and appealing possibilities. But what would happen if I really opened myself to the alternatives suggested. What would happen to my faith? What would happen to my relationships in the community? What would happen to my reputation? What would happen to my livelihood? What would happen to me?

D. Reading this book just enhances my sense of apathy about religion.

I struggled for many years to resolve the problems of the unknown, to develop faith. But now I have given up trying to solve the unsolvable. The only way to live with any tranquility of soul is to give up these hopeless endeavors. The big questions have no answers. Why bother even thinking about them?

I participate in religious ceremonies and rituals. It is a way of engaging a social community. My friends are there. My children go to Sunday school and have a good time. I sing in the choir. Routines are probably of some value. But the intellectual constructs are meaningless, ridiculous and even revolting. I just don't bother thinking about them. It is my observation that there are many people like me.

E. This book provides a framework to look at the New Testament in a creative way.

I live in a society that claims to be Christian. I am well acquainted with the essential elements of the belief system. But my real life is in a scientific world. It is a world of physical and social sciences. My thought life is engaged with the endless analyses of everything. In this kind of a world the historicisms and literalisms of traditional Christianity and modern Christian Fundamentalism fair very poorly. At the very best the dogmas of these kinds of Christianity are not helpful.

The Bible is still a very important book and the term "Christianity" relates to many things and ways of living which I value. These values include such things as caring for people, seeing the essential equality of all human beings, and caring about the earth and the environment.

Traditional Christianity with its dogmas seems to be more interested in a supernatural world and the Gods who supposedly reside there. There is no scientific evidence of such things so I know nothing of such matters. But this does not prevent me from caring about the people and the world in which I live. In fact, I am convinced that a preoccupation with the unknowable supernatural really subverts human responsibility.

The theses of this book provide a rational alternative to the dogmas of traditional Christianity. These theses make a lot of sense to me. For the first time I can read the New Testament with understanding and a great sense of relief. This approach enables people who are "unbelievers" from traditional perspectives to seriously connect or reconnect with Jesus. Jesus did build on the wisdom of the past. He moved us on in the fundamental task of growing into whole and healthy human beings.

This book helps me to recognize the mythical nature of the Biblical materials and earlier scriptures. The myths help me to identify with all peoples, in all places, through all of time. I am part of the human race. I am not unique or special. This lays the foundation to rise above individualism, local loyalties and spiritual exploitation. It helps me to construct meaningful answers for new dilemmas in a changing age.

F. Although this book is on the right track, it doesn't go far enough.

Jesus or Christ? still seems to be concerned about spiritual things. I believe that the way one lives is all that is important. The supernatural world and its Gods are not relevant. Truth for me consists in a loving way of life which helps people grow to their fullest potential.

For me the creeds and dogmas of Constantinian Christianity and its 21st century versions are confusing, irrational, contradictory, misleading, dehumanizing and ultimately degenerative for the human race.

Sacred scriptures of all kinds are confusing and irrelevant to the problems of our day. The myths are distractions with little capacity to inform or reform. I look at the hard realities of human relationships and seek practical answers.

This book, however, gives me pause. I am attracted to the human Jesus presented here. Some elements of his way of life seem relevant to the real world in which I live. The universal ethic of love is understandable and consistent with the best scientific understanding of positive, constructive human relationships. It seems to be a way of life which heals human brokenness. It is a style of life which shows up the futility of solving the problem of violence with violence.

It may be time for me to take a second look at this man, Jesus. Maybe if I took him more seriously it would help me to be more practical in my fundamental commitment to the human race. I might even be able to think of this as the "way of God." In so doing, however, I would be confessing allegiance to a God radically different than the God and the Christ talked about in much of contemporary Christianity.

BIBLIOGRAPHY

Armstrong, Karen – A Short History of Myth; Canongate Books, Edinburgh, 2005

– The Battle for God; Random House, 2000

Campbell, Joseph – The Masks of God: Occidental Mythology; The Viking Press; New York, 1975

– Myths to live By; Bantam Books, New York, 1972

Crossan, John Dominic – The Birth of Christianity; Harper San Francisco, 1999

Duchesne-Guilemin (translated by Henning), – "Wisdom of the East"

Farhand Mehr – The Zoroastrian Tradition; Element Books, (1991)

Fontana, David – The Secret Language of Symbols; Chronicle Books, San Francisco. 1993

Harpur, Tom – The Pagan Christ; Thomas Allen, Toronto, 2004

Homer – The Odyssey

– The Iliad

Kaufman, Gordon – In the Beginning Creativity; Augsburg Fortress Press, Minneapolis, Mn. 2004

– Jesus and Creativity; Fortress Press, 2006

Laughlin, Paul Alan – <u>Remedial Christianity</u>; Polebridge Press, 2000

Manchester, William – <u>A World Lit By Fire</u>; Back Bay Books, New York, 1993

Ovid – <u>Metamorphoses</u>; late first century BCE, translated by Sir Samuel Worth and John Dryden

Pagels, Elaine – <u>Beyond Belief;</u> Random House, New York, 2005

<u>The Book of the Dead</u> – Translated by E A Wallis Budge, 1895

<u>The Pyramid Texts</u>

Sponge, John S. – <u>Why Christianity Must Change Or Die</u>; Harper, San Francisco, 1999

– <u>The Sins of Scripture</u>; Harper, San Francisco, 2005

Taussig, Hal – <u>Jesus Before God</u>; Polebridge Press, Santa Rosa, Ca. 1999

Tuttle, C.E. – <u>A New Christianity For A New World;</u> Harper; San Francisco, 2001

Wenham, David – <u>Paul: Follower of Jesus or founder of Christianity;</u> – Wm B. Erdman Publishing Company, Grand Rapids, Michigan, 1995

FOOTNOTES AND COMMENTS

Chapter 1

[1] H.M. Snider – The Cultural Creation of Christianity – Ch 4

[2] See E.A Wallis Budge – The Gilgamish Epic, the first tablet.

[3] See website shira.net/symbols.htm. The zigguratt was the Mesopotamian version of the Mountain of Heaven, resembling the pyramids of Egypt and Central America in that its summit was a meeting place between deities and mortals. At the peak of the ziggurat the Goddess came down to mate with the king, or the God to mate with the queen. Sumerian towns featured ziggurats as early as 3500 B.C. In Babylon, the ziggurat was the core of the city. Its seven stages were supposed to represent the seven heavenly spheres.

[4] Thotmoses = Moses

[5] Mathew 1:18

[6] Luke 1:35

[7] E.A.Wallis Budge – The Babylonian story of the Deluge and the Epic of Gilgamish

Chapter 2

[8] Some of the material in this chapter is drawn from the text available at website sas.upenn.edu/African Studies/Books/Payrus_Ani. The University of Pennsylvania is a very good source for an introduction to The Pyramid Texts and The Egyptian Book of the Dead as well as many other documents and essays relevant to this Chapter. Access to the work of Budge and the text of the Book of the Dead is most easily accomplished by searching for "Egyptian book of the dead (budge 1895). The materials seem endless. Start with the section The Gods of the Book of the Dead

[9] See website – members.aol.com/egyptart/book. What we call the Egyptian Book of the Dead was known to the Egyptians as "Reu nu pert em hru" which in translation means "The Chapters of coming forth by day." It dates from approximately 1600 BC.

[10] See website – sacred-texts.com/egy/pyt/index.htm. Consult the index.

[11] A translation of these materials was made in 1952 by Samuel A. B. Mercer. The text is available at website – sacred texts.com/Home

[12] See the website – civilization.ca/cicil/Egypt/egcw03e; provides an elementary introduction to the nature of the Pyramid texts and its relationship to The Book of the dead.

[13] Search for the "The Ancient Egyptian Literature" site and select "Annotated Ancient Egyptian Texts." The essays by Charles H. Long are an excellent summary of the main theological ideas of Egyptian Mythology.

[14] See website – shira.net/symbols.htm. Note section "the winged sun disk" Ra here is called the "Sun Of Righteousness with healing in his wings,"

[15] See website – touregypt.net/Godsof Egypt/horus.htm

[16] E.O Faulkner – The Ancient Egyptian Pyramid Texts, 1969 (a few portions have updates as recent as 2006) Note the "Utterance 592 and Utterance 599. Very little of the hieroglyphic material has been translated but at least there are hints of the theology which existed 5 thousand years ago.

[17] See web site – pantheon.org/articles/s/set.html or search for "Osiris" "Seth" for many other sources. All the evidence on the subject now available goes to prove, that the early Egyptians believed that Osiris was a man-God who was murdered and whose body was mutilated., and that various members of his body were reconstituted

[18] E A Wallis Budge. Chapter 5

[19] See website – http://www.touregypt.net/Godsofegypt/horus.htm

[20] See Website – tourguide.net/osirfun.htm; he is called, "Osiris, beloved of his father, the king of the Gods, the lord of life, Osiris."

[21] See website – web.ukonline.co.uk/gavin.egypt/papyrus.htm. It was the hope of every Egyptian to be associated with Osiris in the supernatural world. Note the end of the article "INTRODUCTION TO THE PAPYRUS OF ANI" by Egyptologist Thomas Gibson, 1910

[22] See website – sas.upenn.edu/African Studies/books/Papyrus_Ani.html See Appendix (From the Papyrus of Nu, Brit. Mus. No. 10477, Sheet 22)

[23] See the website – sacred-texts.com/egy/pyt/index.htm; see the pyramid texts ritual of body resurrection, Utterance 21,14b

[24] See the website – webhotep.com The sidebar index will lead you to elaborations of most of the items which I have presented in this section. There are many other websites, providing a large range of materials both scholarly and amateurish and a variety of interpretations and a whole

range of view points. I have attempted to summarize the essence of the most crucial aspects of the Osiris-Horus mythology

[25] Search for "Roman religion" "cult of Isis") select (Greek and Roman Religion). Then select (cult of Isis).

Chapter 3 Persian Theology

[26] Howard M. Snider – The Cultural Creation of Christianity – Chapter 6

[27] Ibid – Appendix E

[28] See website – museums.ncl.ac.uk/archive/mithras/text.

[29] See Roman Mythology, section Foreign Gods at website – wikipedia.org/wiki/Roman mythology

[30] There are innumerable sources for information of the Cult of Mithras. The work by David Ulansky – The Origins of the Mithraic Mysteries; Oxford University Press, 1991 is highly regarded. Among the internet websites relevant to this topic museums.ncl.ac.uk/archive/Mithras/text is probably the most dependable

[31] See H.M. Snider – The Cultural Creation of Christianity – Appendix E

[32] See website – sacred-texts.com/eso/sta/sta04. The Ancient Mysteries and Secret Societies

[33] See website – en.wikipedia.org/wiki/Mithraism – Note article – Mithraism. The content of this article is extensive and one of the most concise summaries of Mithraism I have found. Its contents have been disputed by Constantinian Christians

[34] See website – museums.ncl.ac.uk/archive/Mithras/text; note article – Temple of Mithras

[35] See website – sacred-texts.com/eso/sta/sta04. The Ancient Mysteries and Secret Societies

[36] See website – .museums.ncl.ac.uk/archive/mithras/text.

[37] See website – .museums.ncl.ac.uk/archive/mithras/text – Note articke – Temple of Mithras

[38] See website – sacred-texts.com/eso/sta/sta04. The Ancient Mysteries and Secret Societies

[39] See website – sacred-texts.com/eso/sta/sta04. The Ancient Mysteries and Secret Societies. This seems to be a dependable source relative to this very complex subject. The material here is an extensive discussions on the so called "Mystery Religions" of antiquity and the continuity of many of their elements into Christianity and secret societies. Many of these elements persist in modern Christianity and various "secret societies" such as Freemasons and others.

[40] See article Rome's Basement, National Geographic Magazine, July 2006, page 88

[41] See website – en.wikipedia.org/wiki/Mithraism – Note the picture, its components and location of the scene

[42] See website – mystae.com/restricted/streams/gnosis/Mithra "During...the 'Age of Taurus,' lasting from around 4,000 to 2,000 B.C., the celestial equator passed through Taurus the Bull (the spring equinox of that epoch), Canis Minor the Dog, Hydra the Snake, Corvus the Raven, and Scorpio the Scorpion (the autumn equinox): that is, precisely the constellations represented in the Mithraic tauroctony." – David Ulansey,- The Cosmic Mysteries of Mithras"

[43] See website – well.com/user/davidu/Mithras – This scene shows Mithras in the act of killing a bull, accompanied by a dog, a snake, a raven, and a scorpion; the scene is depicted as taking place inside a cave like the mithraeum itself. This icon was located in the most important place in every mithraeum, and therefore must have been an expression of the central myth of the Roman cult."

[44] David Fontana – The Secret Language of Symbols page 92

[45] See website – museums.ncl.ac.uk/archive/mithras/text – Note article – Temple of Mithras

[46] See footnote 35 in Howard M. Snider The Cultural Creation of Christianity, Infinity publishing, 2005

[47] David Fontana – The Secret Language of Symbols page 92

[48] See website – mystae.com/restricted/streams/gnosis/mithra. Select the ventrue network "A central feature of the ceremonial associated with Mithras was the *taurobolium*, the ritual slaughter of a bull which commemorated and repeated Mithras' primeval act. The initiate was baptized in its blood, partaking of its life-giving properties. It may be noted that this part of the ceremonial closely resembled the ritual of the cult of Cybele, the Great Mother of Asia Minor, which had been brought to Rome three centuries before Christ.."

[49] Web site – world-information.org/wio/infostructure/ "In Hindu mythology, avatars are the form that deities assume when they descend on earth"

[50] Ovid – Metamorphoses Book 2 section – Ocyrrhoe transformed into a Mare – "Old Chiron took the babe with secret joy, proud of the charge of the celestial boy. His daughter too, whom on the sandy shore the nymph Charicle to the centaur bore. With hair dishevel'd on her shoulders, came to see the child. Ocyrrhoe was her name. She knew her father's arts, and could rehearse the depths of prophecy in sounding verse. Once, as the sacred infant she survey'd, the God was kindled in the raving maid. And thus she utter'd her prophetick tale: "Hail, great physician of the world,

all-hail; hail, mighty infant, who in years to come shalt heal the nations, and defraud the tomb; Swift be thy growth! thy triumphs unconfin'd! Make kingdoms thicker, and increase mankind. Thy daring art shall animate the dead, and draw the thunder on thy guilty head: Then shalt thou dye, but from the dark abode rise up victorious, and be twice a God."

Chapter 4 Hebrew Theology

[51] Genesis 11:31. This is the region of modern day Iran and Iraq

[52] See the Chapter "Persian theology"

[53] The creation account of Genesis 1 and 2

[54] Genesis 1:1

[55] Genesis 11:31, 12:1

[56] Genesis 13:18

[57] Genesis 12:10-20

[58] Genesis 14:20

[59] Genesis 21:1-2

[60] Genesis 24:48-51

[61] Genesis 25:21

[62] Genesis 25:34

[63] Genesis 26:6-7

[64] Genesis 30:22

[65] Genesis 45:7-8

[66] Genesis 41:38

[67] Genesis 40:37-45

[68] Genesis 45:7-8

[69] Exodus 7:12

[70] Exodus 19:5-13

[71] Numbers 21:8-9

[72] Deuteronomy 7:6-12

[73] Deuteronomy 7:17:24

[74] Nehemiah 1:5

[75] Genesis 32:28

[76] For further discussion of this topic see Howard M. Snider The Cultural Creation of Christianity; Infinity press 2005, Ch 2

[77] Isaiah 42:7

[78] Amos 5:21-24 and Isaiah 42:1&4

[79] Micah 6:8

[80] See Old Testament Materials; particularly the books of Jonah, Amos and Micah.

[81] This concern for a different kind of social morality occurred in many cultures in the axial and post axial period. See Karen Armstrong – A Short History of Myth; pages 81-83

[82] See the material in Howard M. Snider – The Cultural Creation of Christianity; Infinity Publishing, 2005

Chapter 5 Theology of Asia Minor in the First Century

[83] The material in this chapter is a summary of the materials in the first four chapters. Refer to these chapters for references relevant to the summary ideas.

[84] Concise History of the World, National Geographic Society, 2006, Page 82

[85] Concise History of the World, National Geographic Society, 2006, Page 88

[86] This cross may still be seen in symbols employed in religious literature and stained glass windows of Christian Churches.

[87] Howard M Snider – The Cultural Creation of Christianity, Infinity Publishing, 2005

[88] Ibid

[89] Acts 26:11

[90] Galatians 1:12

[91] The allusions of Paul to the characteristics of the messengers, the Christs of antiquity, in the words used by the religions of antiquity seem almost endless.

[92] See website "Mystae.com/restricted/streas/gnosis/Mithra According to Ulansey [*The Origins of the Mithraic Mysteries* (1989)], Tarsus, an intellectual hub in the first century B.C. and a center of Stoic philosophy, incubated a Mithraic doctrine of cosmic transcendence in response to the discovery of precession by Hipparchus in 128 B.C. To the astrally oriented Stoics, the precessional displacement of the entire cosmos implied the existence of a powerful, unseen God who resided beyond the stars and moved the entire universe according to his own timetable. Ulansey argues this supernatural power was identified in Tarsus with Perseus, the city's legendary founder and divine tutelary hero. Even in the fourth century B.C., Tarsus minted coins depicting Perseus in the company of Apollo and presiding over a lion-bull combat. Ulansey sees Aquarius in the bowl symbol and links it and the lion to the solstices. The

pair of torch-bearing, cross-legged shepherds who so often flank the bull's death scene, he judges, symbolize the two equinoxes."

[93] These conditions are well summarized in The National Geographic The Concise History of the World; edited by Niel Kagan: The National Geographic Society, 2006. The following quotation appears on page 93 "Judea in the first century C. E. was a land rife with political and social tension, between Gentiles and Jews, between Roman overlords and subjects and between various sects of Jews itself. Any man capable of attracting crowds was viewed as politically dangerous by a number of interested parties, Roman governors and Jewish high priests alike, as there was no dearth of Jews ready at a moments notice to begin a holy war against Rome"

[94] See Howard M. Snider – The Cultural Creation of Christianity Ch. 8

[95] Genesis 6:4

[96] Gal 5:22,23

[97] Acts 15:39

[98] Romans 11:13-14

[99] See Laughlins discussion in Remedial Christianity Pages 120-124

Chapter 7 Jesus Christ in the New Testament

[100] Mark 14:22-24, Luke 22:19, Luke 22:42, 1 Corinthians 11:23-26

Chapter 8 Jesus Christ the Only Christ

[101] Marcus Borg

[102] Refer again to the general literary understanding of Myth as described in Chapter 1 of this book and the work of a number of authors listed in the bibliography.

Chapter 9 Salvation and the Nature of Truth

[103] Refer to the works of the Apostolic Fathers, the Ante-Nicene Fathers and the Post-Nicene fathers. Those materials are very extensive. For a elementary and brief introduction to this topic compare the Creeds and their various attempts at the clarification of doctrine.

[104] I Corinthians 1:20-25

[105] The terms "Belief" and "Faith" are not interchangeable. However in creedal and fundamentalistic religions they are used as though they were interchangeable. The term "belief" refers to a condition of mental assent to propositions or dogmas. "Faith" is more properly used in the context

of commitment to a way of life. See Howard M. Snider <u>The Cultural Creation of Christianity</u>, 2005, for more discussion of these terms.

Chapter 10 Jesus or Christ in the Early Church

[106] Luke 1:1-4

[107] Take time to read the Christian Creeds of the first five centuries. Search google for "church creeds" as a beginning point.

[108] Howard M. Snider – <u>The Cultural Creation of Christianity</u>; Infinity Press, 2005, Ch. 5

[109] See Howard M. Snider – <u>The Cultural Creation of Christianity</u> Chapter 8 for a summary description of Constantinian Christianity.

[110] These I have called "Jesus Christians" to distinguish them from "Constantinian Christians" See Howard M. Snider – <u>The Cultural Creation of Christianity</u> Ch 8..

[111] Acts 11:26

[112] Using google search engine find "church fathers" "heretics" This will lead you to a multitude of sources relevant to this topic. It seems that many of the "sainted" church fathers worked vigorously to refute doctrines which were contrary to their own interpretations. Those who held views contrary to the bishops were quickly labeled, "heretics," "schismatics" etc. The Christianity of these heretics was denied and their right to interpret scriptures rejected.

[113] See website – associate.com/library/mirrors/ccel.org/fathers2/ANF-01-56 Note the references to the work of Irenaeus in the Provinces of Gaul early in the second century. Thousands of pages of defense and refutation of positions were written. Viewpoints different from these church fathers is quickly dismissed as heresy. In most cases the work of the "heretics" have been destroyed and what remains of their work are referenced by those who are refuting the "heresy"

[114] See Website – bibleocean.com/OmniDefinition/St._Ireneus This material provides a crude summary of Ireneus theology but it was a theology which set the stage for the next two centuries.

[115] Irenaeus wrote extensively against those who differed from his interpretation of the nature of the body of Jesus Christ. These writings are collected in a work called <u>Irenaeus against Heretics.</u>

[116] <u>Perscriptions against Heretics</u> – Translated by Rev. Peter Holmes. Note the introduction to Chapter 37

[117] St. Augustine – <u>The City of God</u> Book 6 Ch 31

[118] This is my understanding of the way in which Augustine operated.

[119] See Howard M Snider – <u>The Cultural Creation of</u> Christianity – Ch.8

[120] Campbell – The Masks of God, Ch 7, Particularly pages 388ff

[121] See website ondoctrine.com/2catec07.htm for this version. There are many other sources with some variations of the creed.

[122] Christians even into the 5th century engaged in sun worship rituals after Sunday morning worship until such practice was prohibited by Pope Leo

[123] Some of the disciplines represented in these centers of learning are listed in Chapter 5

[124] Consult the internet for "Wikipedia Free Library" and find the article "Library of Alexandria." This is a good beginning point. There is much contradictory material about the destruction of the library. Make your own judgment.

[125] See website – answers.com/topic/hypatia-of-alexandria

[126] Search for "The academy of Plato" "emperor Justinian" "529." Note the reference The Origins of Greek Mathematics.